Finding
Ourselves
in the
Crowd

Finding Ourselves in the Crowd

What 18 Out-of-the-Box Jews Can Teach Us About Individuality in Orthodoxy

GILA MANOLSON

ISBN 978-1-68025-439-6

Typesetting: Michael Silverstein

Printed in Israel

Also by Gila Manolson:

THE MAGIC TOUCH:
A Jewish Approach to Relationships

OUTSIDE/INSIDE:
A Fresh Look at Tzniut

HEAD TO HEART:
What to Know before Dating and Marriage

CHOOSING TO LOVE:
*Building a Deep Relationship
with the Right Person—and with Yourself*

HANDS OFF! THIS MAY BE LOVE:
God's Gift for Establishing Enduring Relationships

In memory of my beloved parents

יעקב הרשל בן ברנרד ודבורה
(Jack Harold Fisch)
and
בלומה פעסל בת נח ושרה
(Beth Paula Fisch)

*for giving me the belief in myself
that underlies everything I do.*

*Even when they didn't agree with me,
they were proud of me.*

OHR SOMAYACH INSTITUTIONS
Tanenbaum College

You are holding an unusual book. Not every Orthodox Jew will see eye to eye with everything in it. I myself disagree with some of its interviewees' statements. Yet it is an extremely important work whose potential for good far outweighs any possible negative response to some of its ideas. It eloquently conveys a message that needs to be heard: the need to discover yourself, to tap into the unique, irreplaceable person that you are, and to make your individuality the foundation of your *avodat Hashem*.

So many people—whether children or adults, *chozrim bit'shuvah* or *"frum* from birth"—lead lives of quiet desperation, squelching their essential selves to conform to a stereotype based more on sociology than on authentic Judaism. As a result, they're stymied and blocked. Some go off the *derech*. Others are left with a perfunctory observance lacking joy, enthusiasm, and passion. There seems to be an either-or choice: Torah or creativity, *frumkeit* or the development of my inner voice. One must invariably be at the expense of the other.

Gila Manolson, a well-respected author whom I personally know as a true *yerei Shamayim*, disabuses the reader of this false dichotomy. On the one hand, she correctly observes that the Torah requires a great deal of conformity: We all must keep Shabbat and kashrut, adhere to the norms of *tzniut*, etc. Furthermore, being part of a community, sharing in its joys and sorrows, is paramount in Yiddishkeit. She also notes that there's no value in being different just for difference's sake. At the same time, she demonstrates that Judaism allows ample room for developing and expressing one's individuality. She does so by profiling 18 men and women fully committed to halachah who have found unique ways to serve Hashem. Many of these stories are extremely moving. The common denominator is that each individual is a whole world. When we don't follow our *neshamah*, that world is effectively destroyed.

In describing the journeys of *B'nei Yisrael* in the wilderness, the Torah attaches tremendous importance to tribal affiliation. Each tribe is counted separately, has its own flag, its own place in the camp, and its own prince, and ultimately receives its own portion in the Land of Israel. At first glance, this particularism is perplexing. We are, after all, one nation with one Torah. What difference does it make if I'm from Reuven, Shimon, or Yissachar? Isn't just being a Jew enough?

There's a profound message here. Yes, we are and must be one nation, but we must simultaneously appreciate the uniqueness of every individual within that nation. Community is not conformity; unity isn't uniformity. Within the tapestry of *Am Yisrael*, each tribe contributes its own distinct color, texture, and nuance, and so does each individual. Only through their blending will Hashem's glory be fully revealed.

Thus, I welcome Gila Manolson's exploration of this fundamental idea. May it help us all discover our own greatness and *kedushah*, enabling each of us to be a true *kiddush Hashem*.

Rabbi Yitzchak Breitowitz
Jerusalem, Israel

Rabbi Yitzchak Berkovits
Sanhedria HaMurchevet 113/27
Jerusalem, Israel 97707
02-5813847

יצחק שמואל הלוי ברקוביץ
ראש רשת הכוללים לינת הצדק
סנהדרייה המורחבת 113/27
ירושלם ת״ו

בס״ד ירושלם ת״ו כ״ב בתשרי תשס״ף

And Hevel, he also brought an offering... (Bereishit 4:4)

Sforno and *Kli Yakar* both see Hevel as unworthy of Divine protection from his brother, Kayin, despite HaSHeM's acceptance of Hevel's sacrifice, as this offering came only as an "also" to Kayin's.

Every Jew possesses a unique *shoresh haneshamah* and is placed in this world to reveal and actualize his own flavor of *avodas HaSHeM*, not merely to copy others.

Commenting on the commandment to write a *sefer Torah*, *Write for yourselves this song* (Devarim 31:19), where the Torah refers to itself as *shirah*, *Torah Temimah* cites a seemingly contradictory Gemara stating that David HaMelech was criticized for calling the laws of Torah *zemiros*. *Torah Temimah* explains that while one shouldn't relate to the Law as mere words of poetry, the beauty of Its fulfillment on a national scale has a songlike harmony. Harmony does, of course, mean everyone singing to the same beat, and yes, the *d'Oraisa*, *d'Rabbanan*, and even *minhag* standardization of service creates the framework for *avodas HaSHeM*. Yet all of that is to be expressed by the individual reaching into the depths of his or her *neshamah* and building his or her personal relationship with HaSHeM and His Torah.

I have known the author for many years and can attest to her integrity in her own *avodas HaSHeM* as well as in her contribution to the *klal* in assisting others in their struggles for growth in Yiddishkeit. There are no hidden agendas to this book, only a sincere desire to inspire us all to make our *avodah* a genuine expression of who we really are and not a lifeless mimicking of people around us.

In expressing individuality, one need not seek out alternatives beyond the consensus, nor must personal expression be obvious to others. In situations where the soul cries out for something very different, one should develop a relationship with a *rav* capable of guiding him or her off the beaten track without severing one's lifeline to the *klal*.

I commend the author on another important work for the mature, intelligent, growth-seeking Jew and wish her many more years of serving the Anglo-Jewish community in her unique ways.

בברכה,

[signature] יצחק ברקוביץ

Contents

Introduction

S EVERAL YEARS AGO, I was asked to speak to a lovely group of Orthodox high school girls on a topic of my choice. At the time, a fashion trend that went against Jewish law was catching on like wildfire in parts of the religious community. What particularly bothered me was how girls (and women) seemed to adopt this new practice unquestioningly. At least give me a good argument why it's okay, I thought. What's this herd mentality? Isn't anyone thinking independently? Isn't anyone an individual? Frustrated, I knew what I wanted to talk to these young women about.

The girls were sitting in a large semi-circle. We smiled at each other. "I'd like to start with just one word," I said. They looked at me curiously. As my gaze swept over the crowd, I cried, "Baaaaa!"

The kids stared at me in shock.

"This," I explained, "is a talk about SHEEP."

Each of us is an individual. We each have our own personalities, our own genes, and our own histories. We each have our own minds, emotions, and natures. We each have our own ways of being and of experiencing the world. Most important, we each have our own souls. And we're free to form our own educated opinions. Discovering and expressing who we are as individuals is part of what God wants from us.

But what does it mean to be an individual? I remember a flyer advertising one of my talks on individuality. It showed a crowd of identical penguins, with one in the middle wearing a big smile—and a large, funky purple hat. Cute. But this image missed the point. First, no matter how identical people may appear, deep down, *everyone* is an individual. There are no clones in God's world. It's just that some people's uniqueness is more obvious than others'. Second, true individuality doesn't mean standing out externally—it means being who you are *internally*. Looking or dressing differently can never define your individuality, it can only reflect it.

Jewish tradition tells us that individuality dates from the revelation of the Torah at Mount Sinai. The Sages teach that when the Torah was given, Moses told each person exactly where to stand in order to witness the event from a unique distance and angle. Every individual experienced revelation differently, emerging with his or her own personal knowledge of God.* Our unique connection to God is the basis of our individuality, including the uniqueness of our own soul, the spark of God within us that wants to shine goodness into the world.

How do we radiate that goodness? God's instructions lie in the Torah, the Jewish guide to making a difference. Just as we each sense and relate to God in our own way, we're each

---

* Sarah Yehudit Schneider, citing *Torah Sheleimah, Yitro*, footnote "*re'u*"; *Mechilta* 19:24, *Mechilta d'Rashbi*; *Zohar* 2:82b.

meant to develop our own perspective (within halachah) on the Torah and its mitzvot, so we can make our own mark on the world.

I think I unconsciously realized the value of individuality in Judaism when I wrote my first book, *The Magic Touch: A Jewish Approach to Relationships*. *The Magic Touch* presented a practical, down-to-earth argument for being *shomer neg-iah*, refraining from physical contact with the opposite sex before marriage. Having lived the first 22 years of my life as a secular Jew, I thought my perspective on this mitzvah might enhance the observance of those raised in religious homes as well as newcomers to Judaism. It turned out I was right. Due to your own unique life path, your "take" on a particular mitzvah might benefit others too.

Even more fundamentally, each of us is drawn to certain mitzvot. Intellectuals may devote themselves to Torah study; contemplative types may connect to prayer; emotional "doers" may find their spiritual home in acts of kindness. Acknowledging our individuality means discovering which mitzvot speak to us most and which we can do best. These mitzvot are our own personal gateway to growth, spiritual satisfaction, and a deep relationship with God.*

Of course, knowing which mitzvot are uniquely ours requires knowing who we are and who we can be. This kind of self-knowledge can be elusive. Yet Chassidic thought points to one time in history when people gained this precious insight. When the Israelites left Egypt and the sea miraculously split, every person there received prophecy—not about

---

* Rabbi Moshe Hauer, citing Maimonides, Commentary to *Mishnah Torah* 3:16.

the future, but about himself or herself. Everyone experienced a personal revelation of why he or she was created and the unique contribution he or she was to make to the world.[*]

This knowledge was available to later generations as well. In the ancient Land of Israel, if someone wanted to understand his or her mission in life, a visit to a prophet could help.

The era of prophecy is long gone, but a glimmer of it remains. At some point in each of our lives, God grants us a holy moment, a vision of the great individual we can become.[**] "Great" needn't mean achieving something extraordinary—there are quieter kinds of greatness, which may go unnoticed by humans but not by God. We must be open to the moment we see the greatness we're destined for and then make it happen.

In this journey toward self-actualization, we need mentors—rabbis, *rebbetzins*, teachers, parents, or anyone steeped in Torah who also understands us. Their purpose is to help us develop our own Torah outlook and find our own Torah path, growing in accordance with the needs of our soul. With this guidance, we can become the great individuals we're meant to be.

So if Judaism promotes individuality, why does Orthodox Jewish life sometimes seem so conformist? Perhaps because some degree of conformity serves a purpose. True self-actualization requires that we be not only individuals

---

[*]   Rabbi Yaakov Haber, citing Rabbi Tzaddok HaKohen, *Tzidkat HaTzaddik*.

[**] Ibid.

with our own goals but also part of a larger group with a larger mission. Conformity strengthens that group identity. It gives us a greater sense of belonging and connection to our community. It keeps us aligned with the people we respect and the values we believe in.

Many mitzvot create precisely this type of constructive conformity. Shabbat is one example. Every Friday before sunset, religious Jews don special attire, light candles, cease creative work, and go to synagogue. Returning home, they recite blessings over wine and bread, eat a festive meal, sing traditional songs, speak words of Torah, and then give thanks for the food they've enjoyed. While customs vary among Jewish communities, we're all celebrating the same day in basically the same way, experiencing a beautiful and powerful oneness with the entire Jewish people.

Yet doing the same thing as Jews all over the world doesn't mean surrendering our individuality. There are no laws governing what clothes we wear on Shabbat (as long as they're modest), what food we eat (as long as it's kosher), or what melodies we sing. This freedom suggests that God wants each of us to celebrate Shabbat our own way—and that's what makes the Jewish world so colorful. My family's Shabbat table, for instance, features a wide range of dress, a whole-food, plant-based cuisine, and—most significant— my husband's original, soul-stirring melodies for *kiddush*, making our Shabbat table uniquely ours.

So both individuality and community are part of our identity. This duality is reflected in our Rosh HaShanah prayers, which describe everyone passing in judgment before God as "*b'nei maron.*" The Talmud translates this enigmatic expression as either a flock of sheep, travelers proceeding single-file along a steep and narrow path, or King David's soldiers. The flock alludes to our all observing the same mitzvot, the travelers to our individuality, and soldiers to how we use that individuality to serve the Jewish people. On Rosh HaShanah we're judged on all three counts, because all are essential to who we are.*

Yes, we are to be "sheeplike" in our basic observance of Jewish law, and we also must be members of a community. Beyond that, we're meant to express our uniqueness, not just for ourselves but for the good of the Jewish nation.

In this book, I tell the stories of 18 out-of-the-box individuals, often in their own words. These Jewish men and women, young and old, range from Chassidic to Modern Orthodox. Some are "*frum*-from-birth," others *ba'alei teshuvah.*

Aside from their commitment to Torah, one thing unites them all: They believe in themselves. They trust the inner voice telling them how to serve God and live Torah. As a result, they experience the profound satisfaction of being true to who they are. And they're changing lives—within their families, their communities, the Jewish world, and the world beyond. They demonstrate how to be yourself within Orthodox Judaism—and how richly rewarding that is.

You may disagree with the beliefs and/or actions of those profiled herein. Some of them may disagree with each other. (Inclusion in this book doesn't imply approval of everyone else in it.) But just as we don't say of people who look different, "What's wrong with them?" we mustn't say that about

---

* Rabbi Dovid Refson, citing Rabbi Elya Lopian.

those who *think* differently.* Diversity gives halachic Judaism its vibrancy. Working to respect our fellow Orthodox Jews, even as we disagree, is part of the challenge of being religious.

No one in this book is trying to stand out—there are no funky purple hats here. Neither are these people trying to prove anything. While they may be "out of the box," they understand that there's no intrinsic virtue in being there (or being "*in* the box," for that matter), only in being authentic. They choose to be themselves. And by hearing about their lives, we can learn to do the same—and to respect everyone else who has made that choice.

I hope their stories inspire you as they have me.

Note:

In quoting the people profiled here, I've retained their Hebrew and Yiddish turns of phrase. (I use a few myself.) If any are unfamiliar, please refer to the glossary at the end of the book.

---

* Kotzker Rebbe.

Chapter One

The Grandmother Who Saved a Life

I'VE ALWAYS FANTASIZED about saving someone's life: A house is on fire, and hearing the cries of a small child through an upstairs window, I race up a ladder and rescue him! A terrorist attack leaves a victim lying bloodied on the sidewalk, and I apply pressure to the wound, preventing her from bleeding to death! Or someone has a heart attack, and I perform life-saving CPR! I've always wanted to experience the indescribable joy of knowing that—aside from my children—someone in this world is alive because of something I did.

I imagine that's how Judith Abrahams feels. Judith is one of those rare individuals who has performed Judaism's supreme mitzvah and the greatest *chesed* imaginable: She has saved a life, which Judaism likens to saving the entire world.[*]

---

[*] Mishnah *Sanhedrin* 4:5.

She had the conviction to do something few people do: She donated a kidney—to a stranger.

Jewish values, *chesed*, and individuality run in Judith's family. Her mother, Pauline, was a strong woman with a fighting spirit. Growing up in Glasgow as one of only two Jewish students in her class (the other was a cousin), Pauline nevertheless maintained a staunch Jewish identity. During World War II, she moved to London and worked for the War Office in two secret units, helping Britain defeat the Germans. Later, in the Army Education Centre, rather than "going through proper channels," she corresponded with soldiers directly in order to better assist them. When her superior reprimanded her, she figured that "the firing squad was an unlikely fate for me" and continued.

Judith's father, Dr. Maurice Gaba, was born in a Welsh mining town. The day after Britain declared war on Germany, he enlisted, feeling this was a war Jews had to fight. Serving on a hospital ship under heavy fire, he repeatedly risked his life. And while docked in Dunkirk, France, he smuggled a Jewish family aboard, bringing them safely to England.

After marrying, Pauline and Maurice (a devoted family physician) were very active in their synagogue and in Jewish causes. Welcoming countless guests into their home, including many Israeli students, the Gabas earned a reputation for hospitality, kindness, and warmth.

Born in 1948, Judith learned from her parents that nothing is more important than being Jewish, performing *chesed*, and standing up for your beliefs. As the only Jewish girl in her class, she also knew what it meant to be different. She stood out in college too, studying biochemistry when few women did. Though married at age 21, she earned her Ph.D. a few short years later.

But it wasn't only academically that Judith followed her own path. Early in their marriage, she and her husband, Alan, went beyond their traditional Jewish lifestyle and began exploring Judaism in depth under the guidance of the brilliant and inspiring Rabbi Dovid Miller, who had come to Glasgow from Gateshead, England. The ethical component of Jewish practice particularly spoke to them. Within a couple of years, they became observant. Having always wanted to make *aliyah*, they now especially yearned for an authentic Jewish life in the Jewish homeland. So in 1976, with one child and another on the way, they moved to Israel.

Fast-forward to 2011. At age 62, Judith was a mother to four adult children and a grandmother many times over, working as a patent agent in the biotech industry and heavily involved in communal activities in Rechovot, where she and her husband had lived since making *aliyah*. Her life was rich and fulfilling. So what made this *bubby* donate a kidney?

One day, Judith's son told her about Rabbi Avraham Ravitz (of blessed memory), a Knesset member promoting a law to encourage altruistic kidney donation (i.e., donating to a non-relative). Rabbi Ravitz himself had needed a kidney and was fortunate to receive one from his son. Yet many patients aren't so lucky. At the same time, most of us are walking around with an extra kidney. "The body can function perfectly well with only one kidney," a leading transplant surgeon in New York told me. "God gave us two so we'd have one to donate."

When Judith heard about altruistic kidney donation, she began researching the issue. Her husband wasn't happy about his wife's interest in donating, but didn't try dissuading her. Judith told very few people about her plan, in case her age would disqualify her from undergoing the procedure.

Judith soon discovered KidneyMitzvah.com, run by Chaya Lipschutz of New York. Herself an altruistic donor, Chaya served as a "kidney matchmaker," bringing together donors and potential recipients nationwide. To donate, Chaya told Judith, she'd need a BMI (Body Mass Index) of under 30—which meant losing weight.

Undaunted, Judith joined a diet and exercise group, shedding 10 kilos (about 22 pounds) in only four months. She was sure Hashem had helped her slim down just so she could donate.

Meanwhile, Judith sought someone in Israel who needed a kidney. Her efforts led her to Matnat Chaim (Gift of Life), an Israeli organization founded by Rabbi Avraham Yeshayahu Heber. Himself a kidney recipient, Rabbi Heber works tirelessly to make kidney matches for others.

Rabbi Heber knew of two sisters, both mothers of large families, who were on dialysis and desperate for a kidney. After extensive medical testing and retesting, Judith proved compatible with the younger sister, age 42, who had endured dialysis three times a week for five years and had so far beaten the high mortality rate. Equally crucial, Judith was deemed healthy enough to donate despite her age. Finally, her dream of saving a life was about to come true.

But not so fast. Although Judith had already been interviewed by a social worker and a psychiatrist, she had to undergo a full psychological examination (with inkblot tests and other psychodiagnostic instruments) to assess her mental stability. Then, along with her intended recipient, she was cross-examined by the Ministry of Health's Transplantation Committee, consisting of yet another social worker and psychologist, a professor of medicine, a lawyer, and others. They fired question after question at her. *Who in her right mind would want to give up a body part to a complete stranger?!* they wanted to know.

Judith could have quoted author Lori Palatnik, another altruistic donor, who realized that if God had given her an opportunity to save someone's life—*anyone's* life—she should grab it. "How can I not give away my kidney, just because it's for someone I don't know?" Lori remarked. "*Somebody* knows them. They're someone's wife, sister, friend, and daughter." Or as donor Jack Doueck wrote: "If someone is in need, no amount of temporary pain can overcome the opportunity to make a difference in the world."

Fortunately, Judith stood her ground, and the Health Ministry gave its approval. And by now, to her immense gratitude, her husband was squarely behind her.

Shortly thereafter, Judith's kidney was removed, and another woman—once a stranger, now a friend—was given a new lease on life.

Although Judith had kept quiet about her impending donation, afterward she heeded her rabbi's advice and went public. Hoping to inspire others to follow her example, she stated: "This saga has been a most amazing experience for me—as joyous and wondrous as giving birth. I am just so grateful to the Almighty that I could do this mitzvah." Indeed, even in the recovery room, though still groggy from the anesthesia, she couldn't stop talking—she was euphoric. Deep down, she still is.

Judith is far from alone in her sentiments. "I've never felt this kind of joy before!" enthused Shari Kaufman, who donated her kidney to a family friend. "My connection with God these past few months is something to strive for the rest of my life. I gave the gift of life and got an equally tremendous gift in return." Yet another altruistic donor told me, "If people knew how amazing it is to donate a kidney, *they'd be lined up to do it.*" This feeling seems to be shared by all kidney donors.

Is there a connection between the idealism and individualism that led a Jewish girl from Glasgow to become religious and make *aliyah,* and that which fueled her altruistic kidney donation? Apparently. Almost all such donors are observant Jews, and many are *chozrim bit'shuvah.*

Though Judith has no more kidneys to donate, she continues donating her time to Matnat Chaim, handling all its English-language correspondence and publications, overseeing its British activities, and guiding English speakers through the donation process.

After Judith's own kidney donation, her oldest daughter dreamed that her mother was about to donate part of her heart. When Judith's recipient heard about this dream, she told Judith, "That's exactly what you did."

Postscript:

In 2016, Judith's son Simcha, 34 and a father of six, followed in his mother's footsteps and donated a kidney. May both Judith and Simcha be blessed to inspire many others.

> When we see 600,000 Jews in one place, we say a blessing declaring God "Chacham harazim," "the Wise One of secrets" (Berachot 58a). This blessing recognizes God's knowledge that, despite our multitudes, we each think differently. Each person's unique views reflect another aspect of His holiness. (Rabbi Asher Meir)

Chapter Two

Using the Wild to Inspire the Child

YOU AND A group of friends are hiking through the woods. Suddenly, out of nowhere, a big black bear appears. It eyes you hungrily and lumbers in your direction. Fortunately, you know not to panic. You and your friends gather together, raise your hands, wave them above your heads, and scream at the top of your lungs. Due to its poor vision, the bear mistakes all of you delicious individuals for one large, threatening blob. Frightened, it quickly retreats about 15 feet. It then turns back at you, reevaluating the situation. Again you all scream, and this time the bear runs off for good.

If you successfully scared off a bear like this—and in the process, learned to face challenges with confidence—it could be because you've gone hiking with Rabbi Tani Prero.

Born in 1979, Tani grew up in Chicago, where a hike was walking to the grocery store, and outdoor survival skills meant shoveling snow off your car. Forests and mountains were the stuff of photographs. Most of his days were spent enjoying the scenery of his suburban neighborhood and yeshivah.

Tani wasn't surrounded by nature, but at home, as the oldest of 11 children, he *was* surrounded by God's other creation: people. "Lots of kids, lots of action," Tani remembers. "By the time I was a teenager, I had learned a lot about how people tick by experimenting on my many siblings." That learning was to pay off in the future.

Tani's adolescence was tough. While he humorously refers to these years as his "teen angst," the truth is, he was searching—for his own connection to God and Torah, and for himself.

Tani's search landed him in Israel, in Yeshivat Sha'alvim. There his love for Torah study was sparked. "The rabbis created an environment in which I felt comfortable asking questions," he says. "Everyone was excited about learning, and there was a spirit of healthy spiritual exploration." In his two years at Sha'alvim, Tani came into his own as a religious Jew.

At the same time, a new piece of his identity started forming. Sha'alvim introduced Tani to the great outdoors. Whether hiking in the forest-covered hills between the yeshivah and Jerusalem or in the Judean desert, Tani loved being out in nature. "I felt good breathing the air and seeing the grass, trees, flowers, water, and animals," he remembers. God's world was impressing itself upon Tani's soul.

By the time he returned to the U.S. and began attending the Yeshiva of Greater Washington, Tani was becoming an avid outdoorsman. When he wasn't in the *beit midrash*, he could be found hiking the Great Falls along the Potomac. "It was just amazing being in such beautiful natural surroundings," Tani recalls. "Like being in shul, there were no loud voices, no music, no distractions. I felt awe and peace. It was a kind of *hitbodedut*—just being alone with Hashem."

Working as a camp counselor during the summer, Tani realized he had a flair for helping and teaching teenagers. So after receiving his B.A. in Talmudic Law, he got a Master's in Education through the Jewish Educational Leadership Institute at Loyola University. Torah, the outdoors, and people—the three strands of Tani's identity were coming together.

Then the life-changing event occurred: He made a connection with Rabbi Zev Freundlich, whose Ya'alozu ("They Shall Be Merry") wilderness adventure camp in the Catskills inspired boys to discover their own strengths while experiencing God through the beauty of the world.

Recognizing his talents, Rabbi Freundlich appointed Tani head counselor. The rabbi taught him about wilderness survival, education, and how to motivate and inspire kids. At the end of the summer, Rabbi Freundlich sent a group of campers on a 10-day hike with Tani as their guide. "I had gone on only one overnight hike in my life," Tani recounts, "and there I was hiking for 10 days straight, sleeping in the woods every night." That trek, more than anything, impressed upon Tani how inspiring the wilderness was.

Rabbi Freundlich, on his part, was so impressed by Tani that he turned the entire camp over to him.

As the new camp director, Tani felt he needed to hone his wilderness survival skills. Back in Israel, he joined a group of young men led by ex-marine David Stern, who took them to the forests outside of Safed. There, for an intensive two months, Tani learned how to build fires, navigate a mountain without trails, stalk and track wildlife, use parts of dead animals as tools, and understand the language of birds. He practiced splatter vision ("owl eyes"), training himself to focus not on one point but on an entire field of vision. And walking meditations opened his eyes to many more living creatures than he'd ever seen.

But Tani didn't just love the wilderness—he understood its healing power. So after marrying at age 27, starting *semichah* studies, and making *aliyah*, he enrolled in a two-year Kibbutzim College course in wilderness adventure therapy. There—as the only student who spoke not of "nature" but of God—he learned about emotional difficulties and how to use the beauty and challenge of the wilderness to ease them.

Tani brought this knowledge back to his camp, which he renamed Yagilu, "They Shall Rejoice," expressing the great joy to be experienced in the great outdoors.

More than just getting boys out into nature, Yagilu gives them the growth experience of a lifetime by immersing them in the wonders of God's world. High-schoolers go hiking, white water rafting, caving, and rock climbing. They learn to make fires, use ropes and knots, carve wood, make tools, build shelters, orienteer and navigate, camouflage themselves, signal when they're lost, recognize stars and what they can tell us—and, of course, scare away bears. They learn how to survive even extreme circumstances. Perhaps most important, they develop belief in themselves.

"I once took my campers on a two-day mountain hike," Tani recounts. "One rather chunky kid felt he wasn't up to it. He was so nervous and fearful that he got dizzy, tripped, and fell. 'I'm too fat, I'm too weak, and I can't do this!' he moaned. 'I'm gonna die!' I deliberately chose another insecure boy and told him, 'You have ten minutes to explain to him why he can do it.' Ten minutes later, they were climbing the mountain together. Years afterwards, the heavy kid told me this incident was a turning point in his self-confidence. And the other boy realized he could make a difference."

In addition to wilderness experience, Yagilu offers its Farm program, in which boys farm and care for animals. And in Yagilu's Nature program, younger campers learn to identify edible plants, build bridges and dams, fish, catch frogs, and tell time by the sun.

Through Yagilu, Tani has taught close to 1,000 boys not only survival skills but crucial life skills, such as leadership, teamwork, and how to set goals and work toward them. Under his creative directorship, Yagilu encourages kids to be happy and self-aware not only in the wilderness but in relationships—by listening, understanding, and respecting one another. Seeing its results, some are even trying to copy his model in their businesses.

As a wilderness therapist, Tani also works one-on-one. "A father once contacted me about his son, who was smart and capable but totally unmotivated and often unwilling even to get out of bed. It had become a struggle to get him to go to school or do anything else.

"I took them on a father-son bushwhack hike. The boy was intrigued by his surroundings and asked a lot of questions. The father, a brilliant man with several advanced degrees, had answers for everything. The youngster was left with no way to express open-ended curiosity and wonder, or to learn and discover on his own.

"I knew the boy needed his space, so I encouraged him to 'blaze the trail' by running ahead. Then, alone with his dad, I explained why I'd separated them.

"He stopped being a know-it-all and learned instead to say, 'That's a great question! What do you think?' And his son regained his motivation."

Tani also teaches kids to love being physically active in nature. "The *neshamah* needs Torah, but the body needs activity," Tani notes. "The Sages' prescription of '*Torah im derech eretz*' ['Torah with the way of the world'] can be understood as saying that the Torah should be combined with physical labor."*

In short, we have bodies and they need to move. Someone once objected to my describing myself as "addicted" to exercise. "Are you 'addicted' to water?" she commented. "Are you 'addicted' to air?" Exercise, she was saying, is just as essential.

Tani sees no better place to move our bodies than in the great outdoors. Sadly, many children today grow up lacking contact with nature. In his book *Last Child in the Woods: Saving Our Children from Nature-Deficit Disorder*, Richard Louv quotes a fourth-grader as saying, "I like to play indoors better, 'cause that's where all the electrical outlets are." According to Louv, playing all day on a smartphone instead of in a creek is directly linked to child obesity, Attention Deficit Disorder (ADD), and depression.

Our need for nature is not just physical and psychological, but spiritual. "All our lives, we're in human-created spaces," Tani points out. "We live in homes built by people, work in buildings built by people, and drive on roads paved by people in cars manufactured by people. But when we go out into nature, we're in the world God created, as He created it. We can connect to the original energy He put into the world, and to Him."

Although Tani's spiritual path differs from that of most people, his *rebbe*, Rabbi Ahron Lopiansky, has encouraged him every step of the way. "People say that Tani's out of the box, and it's not easy to debate that," he says with a smile. "But in truth, most people's boxes are really compartments

---

* See Maharal, *Derech Chayim, perek 2, mishnah 2.*

in a bigger box." In other words, "boxes" become less significant when we widen our vision.

Tani makes an additional point about being different. "I don't like being called 'out of the box,' because I don't see why people have to look over their shoulders to see what others are doing. A parent once asked me what kinds of snacks the other boys brought to camp, so her son could bring the same ones and not feel self-conscious. I told her he should bring what he likes, because we don't judge people by their snacks."

People don't always know what to do with Tani's passion for the great outdoors. Some poke fun at him. "I'll ask someone for something, and he'll say, 'You're a survival guy—go find it in the woods.' Or people joke about my personal hygiene, since I 'live in the forest.'" Others keep their distance. "Some people are scared of the wilderness, so they're scared of me. But some are just scared of expressing who they are. I feel bad for them—and frustrated that society punishes individuals."

Then there's the outright criticism. "Sometimes people would get upset at me for thinking and acting independently," Tani says. "They'd warn me, 'You'll never get married. You won't be accepted in a community. You won't be able to earn a living.'" Tani proved them wrong: He's happily married and part of a wonderful religious community where people appreciate him, and his livelihood brings him tremendous satisfaction. In following the call of his soul, Tani has fused love of God and Torah, love of the wilderness, and love of people in a unique and powerful way.

Tani currently lives with his family in Mevo Horon, near Modi'in, and teaches at Yeshivat Torah V'Avodah. In addition to leading wilderness adventures in Israel, he travels internationally, giving workshops in group dynamics, team building, and leadership, providing educational consulting and parental coaching, and training therapists, teachers, parents, and administrators. And he's constantly expanding Yagilu with his fresh thinking.

"When I express my own ideas, usually about parenting or schooling, people tell me I'm a creative thinker," says Tani. "I don't know why. When I see a problem that needs to be solved, I simply consider all the options, including unconventional ones. I once said that instead of medicating so many ADD kids so they can adapt to school, maybe we should medicate the schools to adapt them to our children's needs. But I'll accept being called a creative thinker, as long as people mean it as a compliment."

How has Tani's pursuit of his own path affected his relationship with God and Torah? "It's how I learn, it's how I daven," he answers simply. "I am who I am. If I tried to be someone else, I wouldn't be serving God. It would be a kind of *avodah zarah*.

"People have actually asked me, 'Why do you have to be different?' I never tried to be different. I think I was just born that way. And I'm learning to enjoy it more and more."

POSTSCRIPT:

Tani's love for God and Torah ignited Jewish souls even in the secular Kibbutzim College. Hiking in the Judean Desert, he told a classmate named Shai about a blessing he particularly loved, said when beholding a beautiful view: "Blessed are you, Hashem, our God, King of the world, *shekachah lo ba'olamo* [Whose world is just so]." As Tani explained,

> Sometimes beauty is beyond words. The second we begin to describe beauty of magnitude, we shrink the beauty into our own words and concepts. Instead of feebly attempting to apply descriptive terminology to the scene, this *brachah* simply states that this is how it is in [God's] world. We praise Hashem and His world, but without daring to make it ours. It's His world, and it's just so.

Shai was moved. At their first opportunity, he and Tani recited the blessing together. Shai then told another hiker, Ron, about it. The next day, encountering another stunning view, Tani helped Ron say the blessing. Tani shares what happened later:

> Further on the hike [...] was a breathtaking view of the Dead Sea and the surrounding mountains [...]. While everyone was at one side of the canyon, Ron stood alone on the other. Out of the corner of my ear, I heard someone yelling.
>
> Some experiences are so gripping, and the responses so raw and real, they burn their way into your mind forever. The interaction, the rendezvous between man and Creator that I witnessed there, etched itself into the rocks, water, sun, and clouds, and into the hearts of all who witnessed it.
>
> I turned to see Ron [...], fist raised, pounding the air and exclaiming over and over, "*Shekachah lecha ba'olamcha* [Your world is just so]!"

In Genesis 1:27, the Torah tells us: "So God created Adam in his image, in the image of God he created him." "In his image" means that, before God created Adam in His image, He created Adam in Adam's own image. (Rabbi Joseph B. Soloveitchik)

Chapter Three

(Wo)man's Best Friend

THE YEAR IS 2017. It's a sunny afternoon at the Weiss home in Cleveland. As she frequently does, Rivky Weiss is hosting two or three dozen guests, none invited. But they haven't come for a Shabbat or holiday meal. Rather than sitting around the dining room table, they're out in Rivky's small yard, playing with puppies. Rivky Weiss is teaching her neighbors to love dogs.

Rivky was born in 1981, the third child out of four and the only daughter. She spent her early years in Nova Scotia, on rural Cape Breton Island.

"Before they married, my parents were hippies," Rivky relates. "They had a guru, practiced Indian-style religion, meditated, and even spent time in an ashram. But their Jewish spark was never quite extinguished.

"When we were traveling around, we sometimes stayed with my father's cousin in Massachusetts, who had become *frum*. There we got to experience Shabbos. She and her husband also sent my parents Jewish books. Slowly, my parents began adopting a few Jewish customs. They started lighting candles on Friday before sundown. They stopped working on Saturdays and didn't let us answer the phone before noon. And they would read about the *parashah* from the children's book *The Little Midrash Says*. At some point, they began feeling they didn't want their children to intermarry. But they realized that if they stayed in Nova Scotia we probably would. That's when they decided to seriously check out Judaism."

When Rivky was in second grade, her family moved to what felt like a huge city—Providence, Rhode Island. Her parents soon became active members of its small Orthodox community. Rivky was sent to the Providence Hebrew Day School—a rather jarring change from her French-speaking public school in Nova Scotia, but she adjusted.

Rivky always loved and wanted to work with animals. By age 11, she knew exactly what she wanted to do with her life. "I didn't feel I had the smarts to be a veterinarian, and I honestly wasn't that interested in being one," she remembers. "But then I read a book about a blind boy who got a seeing eye dog. It made me realize there were other animal-related fields out there, and they sounded really interesting. I decided I wanted to train dogs."

The summer after 10th grade, Rivky landed her dream job: head zookeeper at Camp Sternberg, an Orthodox Jewish summer camp in the Catskills. "My staff and I oversaw the care of the animals and ran activities for the bunks," she explains. "I got guidance from Liz Kaufman, a veterinarian from Jerusalem's Biblical Zoo who came to Camp Sternberg every summer. After the first four weeks, Liz would leave, so I took over. I guess Liz liked me, because when I went to Israel during 11th-grade winter vacation, she created a volunteer program for me at the zoo. I continued at Camp Sternberg for the next two summers. I loved it."

After high school, Rivky decided to spend a year at a seminary in Israel. While her career plans were set, her Judaism was less so. "I hadn't yet found my place in the religious Jewish world," she says. "I needed to figure out my *hashkafah*." Unfortunately, the seminary Rivky attended wasn't the place to do it. But she spent nearly every Shabbat with Liz and her husband, Joe, who became not only surrogate family but good friends and spiritual advisers.

Upon returning from Israel, Rivky moved to New York City to pursue her passion. For half a year, she worked at "the premier doggie day care facility on the Upper East Side," Biscuits and Bath Doggie Gym. "It was the first facility of its kind, and it was awesome," Rivky recounts. "I worked the desk and sometimes also the play yard, which is what I loved most. It was a great job. There was a possibility of advancement, but it would have meant not dealing directly with the dogs, which is what I wanted to do." While working there, she attended night school at Sara Schenirer College, studying behavioral sciences, which she was told would be helpful for dog training.

After a few months, however, Rivky sensed something essential in her life was missing. "I still didn't know what kind of observant Jew I wanted to be," she says. "But then I suddenly realized that I had no clue if I wanted to be observant at all! What I did know is that if I was going to be religious, I wasn't going to do it halfway. I needed to know where in Judaism I belonged and then fully be the person I felt I was meant to be."

Rivky went back to Israel, but this time she enrolled in a seminary for *ba'alot teshuvah*. "Being there was the hardest thing I've ever done," she admits. "I had to examine and question myself from the bottom up, trash the parts of me I no longer wanted, and develop brand-new parts. It was unbelievably intense. I loved every minute of it." At the same time, she benefited from down-to-earth guidance from the Kaufmans and other mentors. "Thanks to both the seminary and the wonderful people I spent time with in Israel," she says, "I found myself."

At age 22, Rivky married Dan, a *ba'al teshuvah* with a background in entertainment. The couple initially stayed in Israel so Dan could continue learning in yeshivah. Two years later, first child in tow, they returned to the U.S. and settled in Cleveland. Dan began studying for his MBA, and Rivky apprenticed with a clicker trainer.

"Clicker training uses positive reinforcement based on psychologist B. F. Skinner's operant conditioning, which means teaching through reward," Rivky explains. "Traditional animal training is punishment- and force-based—pushing an animal into position, jerking a leash, and using fear. But back in the 1970s, a marine mammal trainer named Karen Pryor figured out clicker training, which she used to train porpoises. The clicker makes a clear, sharp sound, kind of like when you press the metal cap on a jar. First you teach them that a click means a treat. Then you use the click to mark the moment the animal has done the right thing. For instance, if you're training an animal to sit, when its bottom hits the ground, you click, add a voice cue—'good sit!'—and give a treat. That's how you begin training the animal to do what you want."

Rivky was enthralled with clicker training. "It made me giddy," she says. "Using positive reinforcement with dogs—or any animal—is magical. Because there's no force or punishment, the dog can choose whether to participate. If it's not interested, the trainer can either make the 'game' more interesting or try again later. The dog can also decide, 'Hey, I'd like some treats, attention, affection,' initiate appropriate contact with the handler, and behave in order to receive what it wants. I'm not even sure I can articulate what this two-way communication between a human and an animal feels like."

In 2016, Rivky opened her own dog training business. Her clients were pet owners, breeders, and people who wanted specialized support in animal training.

"All trainers have a slightly different list of basics," Rivky says. "When I get a new puppy, I work on 'sit,' 'down,' 'stay,' and 'go to your bed.' There's 'recall'—having the dog come to you when called, which signals reliability and is important not only in everyday life but for safety. Then there's 'crate'—teaching the dog to relax in its crate when home alone or traveling. Then, of course, there's potty training. I also teach loose-leash walking, wearing a collar, being in a home, and other skills. Finally, I work on adjustment to a suburban environment and socialization—with other dogs and, most important, with people.

"You know how kids are more cooperative when you speak quietly instead of yelling? Well, the same goes for dogs. My approach is to be gentle and calm."

Rivky has had up to four live-in trainees at a time plus another five to seven just boarding. "I once took in a French bulldog named Bruno who had bitten his owners' kids," she recalls. "I identified the behavior causing the biting, and over three weeks, I turned him around and gave them back an excellent, calm, and happy family dog. Successes like that make my work so rewarding."

In 2018, the Weisses and their four children made *aliyah* to Ramat Beit Shemesh, along with their dog, Sunny, an adorable Labradoodle (a cross between a Labrador and a poodle). "Sunny sat at my feet for the entire 12-hour flight," Rivky recounts proudly.

Once in Israel, Rivky renewed her interest in training service dogs. "There's an extremely wide range of service animals and what they can offer," she says. "There are seeing eye dogs for blind people, hearing dogs for the deaf, seizure alert dogs, and diabetic alert dogs. There are arson dogs, bomb- or drug-sniffing dogs, and mobile assist dogs. Dogs are being tested for their disease- and cancer-smelling abilities. There are also therapy dogs, which can help with autism, PTSD, depression, and anxiety. All this from an animal that lacks judgment or malice and is full of love. Dogs are really miraculous beings!"

Animal-assisted therapy needn't involve only dogs, Rivky adds. Petting other animals as well is calming, and snuggling with them releases oxytocin, which aids in healing.

"Religious Jews often don't understand the therapeutic benefits of being around something with no expectations of you," she says. "If you take good care of an animal, it loves you. It's that simple. Many people, including my own clients, have gotten a therapy dog for a child, and it's ended up benefitting the entire family. Even in my home, we've experienced this phenomenon. When I got Sunny, my husband was less than thrilled—dogs can be a real expense. But now he sees how great it is to have her. When he's stressed, he loves to pet her. And when my kids are hurt or upset, they cuddle with her. Dog therapy works wonders."

Rivky seems well on her way to establishing herself in Israel. "I've met the head trainer of the Israel Guide Dog School, which does the same training I do, and I toured this amazing facility," she relates. "I'm also really looking forward to the next ClickerExpo, an incredible three-day conference for clicker trainers, so I can bring everything I learn back to Israel. But my immediate goal is to improve my Hebrew, so I can become a guide dog mobility instructor."

Meanwhile, Rivky is continuing her regular dog training. "I recently had such an amazing session, it made everything I do worthwhile," she says. "Dory, approximately 1½ years old, had been rescued from an animal shelter. Her owners were very frustrated because any time company came to their small apartment, she would bark her head off. They felt they could no longer have guests.

"As soon as I walked in the door, she was uncomfortable. But by turning my back to her and using other calming body language, I communicated that I wasn't a threat. The family was amazed she wasn't barking. We discovered that the usual way people befriend dogs—putting a hand out to be sniffed, speaking gently, or patting—was exactly what was stressing Dory out. She just needed to be ignored! It was so exciting to go into this home and solve a problem that could have resulted in people giving up their dog."

Much of the Orthodox world aren't comfortable around dogs. Rivky offers a few reasons. "Many Holocaust survivors are afraid of these animals, having experienced vicious attack dogs, and they seem to have passed that feeling down. Also, Jews who immigrated to the U.S. initially lived in cramped, urban quarters that didn't lend themselves to dogs, so they were never part of life. Today as well, not all parents of a large family want or can afford another dependent creature. So culturally, many Orthodox Jews don't know how to interact with dogs. That can lead to bad experiences—and fear."

Rivky tries to reduce that fear and show people how to behave around dogs. "While I was starting my training business, I ran a *chug* for *frum* children in the neighborhood," she reports. "I wanted to teach them the skills that would not only keep them and the dogs safe, but allow them to enjoy each other. When people are afraid, they naturally scream and run away, which for a dog is a call to play. So then you have a terrified kid being chased by a dog that's just looking for some fun! In the *chug*, the children got to hang out with puppies, learn how to interact with them, and even train them in a few basic skills. One little girl who at first needed to be held the entire session got to the point where she could pet a puppy. It was fantastic. I loved transforming how *frum* kids felt about dogs.

"Once I got busy with training, I didn't have time to run the *chug* anymore, but kids kept knocking on my door. On any given weekend, I had 20 children and their parents either playing with the puppies in my yard or watching them through the gate. The parents were thrilled that their kids weren't scared of dogs—even though they themselves often were! It was great that they wanted to free their children of that fear."

How has the *frum* community as a whole related to Rivky's work?

"When I was single, someone asked me how I thought I'd ever get married given my love for dogs," she says. "I certainly did have *shidduchim* experiences where I was considered too 'out of the box.' But that never kept me from doing my thing.

"We were known in Cleveland as a 'different' kind of family. We're fairly 'crunchy granola'—we're mostly vegan, we've homeschooled our kids on and off, I wear colorful clothing and headscarves, we used cloth diapers, we have non-Jewish friends, and more. So people saw the dogs as just another part of that.

"All in all, people think what I do is either cool, interesting, or scary, depending on how frightened or not frightened they are of dogs. But they're always fascinated."

Has Rivky and Dan's "crunchy granola" image followed them to Israel? "I have no clue," she says with a shrug. "We're trying to be growth-oriented Jews, raise our kids in such a way that, God willing, we'll have excellent relationships with them, and get close to Hashem and serve Him as best we can. Isn't that what's important?"

Has Rivky encountered any outright opposition to her passion for dog-training? "Not that I've ever noticed," she says, "but I tend not to notice stuff like that."

Finally, how does Rivky feel about being "out of the box"?

"I don't think about it so much. I just do what my *neshamah* needs to do while staying in the 'box' of halachic Judaism. I try pretty hard to not be a '*davkanik*,' just a normal Orthodox Jew. And to me," she adds, "'normal' means caring primarily about Torah, not about things that don't matter—like whether people are 'different.'"

> In Psalms 147:4, we read: "He counts the number of stars and calls them all by their names." A name represents uniqueness. If God recognizes stars as unique, all the more so human beings. (Rabbi Jonathan Sacks)

Chapter Four

The Courage to Speak Up

THERE ARE COUNTLESS ways of helping people. We can donate time or money to a worthy cause, lend a hand with a difficult task, or simply cheer up a bedridden neighbor. But sometimes making a difference in another's life starts with just noticing something and having the courage to speak up.

Rachel Blume* is a young woman with a special story. It all began with her upbringing in Jerusalem.

"My home was very warm and caring," Rachel recalls. "My parents were involved in *kiruv*, and we had Shabbos guests from all over. My folks welcomed everyone, including people from difficult and traumatic backgrounds, and tried to help however they could. Consequently, I always befriended girls who had struggles in their lives. I felt proud

---

* Not her real name.

of how Jews regard each other as family, and I developed a passionate connection to *Am Yisrael*.

"My parents also gave us a lot of self-confidence. Although they pretty much 'mainstreamed' themselves to fit into our largely *charedi* neighborhood, we saw that they were individuals and believed in our individuality. They didn't impose one way of being religious—their approach was that as long as you're following halachah and a reputable rabbi, you should be free to find your own path in Torah and in life. My *hashkafah* stayed basically *charedi*, but in other ways, I took my own direction. Compared to other girls in my community, I was a bit 'wild and crazy.' People said I had a 'big' personality. And I voiced my opinions when I felt strongly about something. In other words, I was pretty different from many of my Bais Yaakov classmates.

"Because of how I was raised, I learned two major things: to care about others, and to believe in myself. When it comes to helping people, I'm not afraid of doing whatever needs to be done or saying whatever needs to be said. I've resolved never to be passive or silent."

When Rachel was 19, that resolve was put to the test.

One evening, Rachel was leaving the Jewish Quarter of Jerusalem's Old City. Eschewing her usual route, she detoured to an area overlooking the Kotel and sat down on a bench to take in the inspiring view.

Opposite her, at a distance, sat a young couple. Glancing at them, Rachel recognized the man as an Arab employee in a nearby institution where she had recently volunteered. He recognized Rachel as well. Grinning at her, he began playing with his girlfriend's hair. Seeing Rachel watching them, the girl looked uncomfortable. Suddenly Rachel realized that she knew her as well, from the gym—and she was Jewish. She and the young Arab man were holding hands.

Rachel froze. She had heard of Jewish girls becoming involved with Arab men, living with them in their villages, even marrying and having children with them. Typically from low-income, troubled backgrounds, these girls were desperate for love. Upon moving into an Arab village, their freedom was often severely curtailed. Sometimes they were abused. In the worst cases, they became virtual captives and had to be rescued clandestinely.*

Rachel knew she had to do something. But what?

"Before we go, would you buy me some gum?" she heard the girl coyly ask her companion.

He readily rose and headed off in search of a store.

Rachel realized this might be her only opportunity to speak to the girl alone, and she had to seize it.

"I was shaking a little," she admits. "But how could I let her walk away?" Rachel took a deep breath and approached her.

"Hi!" she said to the girl with a smile.

The girl—whom I'll call Shira—looked at her in surprise.

Rachel knew she had very little time. Somehow, the right words just came to her. "Is everything okay?" she asked gently, warmth and concern in her eyes.

Rachel couldn't have expected what happened next. As if a dam burst, Shira broke down and began crying.

"It was a very vulnerable moment," Rachel recalls. "I didn't want her to feel judged. I wanted her to know I was there for

---

* This is not to stereotype Arabs, just to describe the unfortunate reality of some.

her. Only later did I realize what a turning point this was for her. No one else had shown her they cared. When someone finally did, she was suddenly forced to face herself and ask, 'What's going on? What am I doing??'"

Rachel sat down next to her. Through her tears, Shira told Rachel how unhappy she was. Her home life was miserable. Her parents mistreated her. She had no friends. But this man gave her attention. He drove her places. He bought her things. He made her feel loved. As Shira wept, Rachel tried her best to comfort her.

Finally Shira started to calm down. Rachel knew the next step she had to take. Looking Shira in the eye, she spoke from her heart: "If you want a boyfriend, we'll try and find you a Jewish one. And if you have no friends, *I'll be your best friend.*"

Shira looked surprised—then grateful.

"C'mon," Rachel said, putting her arm around Shira. "Let's go."

But before they could, the Arab returned. He eyed them suspiciously. "I knew he guessed what we'd been talking about," Rachel recounts. "And I was afraid he'd either try to get rid of me or pull Shira away." Standing over them, he scowled at Rachel, who had taken his seat. She was scared but didn't get up. He kept glaring at her.

Just then an older man approached and spoke to the young man in Arabic. From his gestures and tone, Rachel understood that he was telling him to get back to work. Reluctantly, the young Arab turned to go, but not before giving Rachel an angry parting look. Then he left. The two girls were blessedly alone again.

"You're coming home with me," Rachel told Shira. "We'll take care of everything." Shira wiped away her tears, and the two caught the first bus to Rachel's house.

At home, Rachel gave Shira something to eat and set up an extra bed for her in her bedroom. Meanwhile, Rachel privately told her mother what had transpired that evening.

"Call my friend Esther,*" her mother told her. "She works with an organization called Learn and Return. She can help."

The next morning, Rachel accompanied Shira to Learn and Return's office. Esther took Shira out to lunch, where they talked about her life and her future. After a few such meetings, Shira began realize what she already knew deep inside—she had to break up with the Arab. Not long afterward, bolstered by Esther and Rachel, she terminated the relationship.

Esther and Rachel were in touch with Shira for several months, providing constant support and guidance. Whenever she was tempted to backslide, they strengthened her. When they found out her cell phone still contained the numbers of many Arab men she could call whenever she needed a ride, they offered her a new phone, which she accepted. Most important, when she was ready, they arranged for a counselor to help explore her emotional issues.

In time, Rachel learned more about Shira's family situation. When warned of Arab men abusing their wives and girlfriends, Shira countered, "So what? My father and my brothers hit me—what does it matter if it's my boyfriend?" Suddenly Rachel understood how at-risk Shira was.

---

* Not her real name.

Little by little, Shira started getting her life on track—and being less in touch with Rachel. "It was uncomfortable for her to be reminded of that period in her life," Rachel explains. But Shira texted her that she'd had moved into an apartment with some nice girls, enrolled in college, and was starting to date Jewish boys.

Shira eventually got engaged to a religious guy. He was healthy and stable—as was she. Rachel joyfully attended their wedding. "I was probably the only one there who knew what a milestone it was," she says. A couple of years later, Shira sent Rachel a picture of her holding the couple's first child—and smiling.

Rachel sees a connection between her being different and her willingness to speak up and help Shira. "I hope any caring person would have done what I did," she notes. "But I think it's easier to rise to that kind of challenge if you're not like everyone else, so you've had to learn to believe in yourself. Being different forced me to develop an inner strength, and that's how I could step in and intervene in a stranger's life."

Has Rachel gotten flack for being different? "Only from a few people," she says. "My high school principal subtly tried to get me into the *charedi* 'mold.' It didn't work. And in seminary, one rabbi told me I have to choose which world to fit into. I told him I'm fitting into Hashem's world.

"Although I still believe in that ideal, I see that in reality it doesn't always work. At least in Israel, once you're married and enroll your child in a certain school, you have to fit in there. I hope things change, but if they don't by the time I have school-age children, I'll do what I have to do. In the meantime, it feels good not to worry about conforming.

"Of course, being different makes dating more difficult, because I need a different kind of man. But if Hashem created me, he created my soul mate too, and I'll find him. And the only way to do that is to be myself."

I asked Rachel about the pros and cons of being different. "The biggest pro is that, instead of feeling connected to society's expectations of you, you feel connected to yourself. This leads to a deeper love for Hashem, because when you appreciate your own uniqueness, you appreciate how beautifully and uniquely He created each and every one of us. The biggest con is that sometimes people look down on you. But I can live with that."

After Shira's story, Rachel wanted to help others with difficulties. She began by working with girls from traumatic backgrounds, then with juvenile delinquents. She builds them up so they can overcome their behavioral issues, many of which stem from low self-esteem. Her own self-confidence has made her a role model for these young people. "Hashem has blessed me with the strengths necessary to work in this field," she says, "and that's where I want to make my mark."

Meanwhile, Rachel has already saved one Jewish girl—just by finding the courage to speak up—and she hopes to save many more.

> The menorah in the Temple—the light we shine back to God—must be molded from a single block of gold. Nothing can be attached. Whatever we are to become must be shaped from who we already are. (Sarah Yehudit Schneider)

Chapter Five
One Step at a Time

"[A woman] must worship God with all [her] faculties, as the Psalmist says: 'All my bones shall proclaim, O God, who is like unto You?' (Psalms 35:10). [...] If one was endowed with grace and ability, one should dance before God." — Rabbi Abraham Twersky

MICHELLE PENN, BORN in 1988, was blessed with parents who encouraged their children's self-development in every way. From the time she entered preschool, she was tirelessly chauffeured to and from an endless array of activities in her Fort Lauderdale community. One of these—which she began at the tender age of 3—was dance. "Dance was the one thing I never stopped," she recounts. "I studied ballet, tap, and jazz, and I totally loved it. Even with everything else I participated in—soccer, swimming, diving, piano lessons, you name it—dance always had a special place in my heart."

So did being Jewish. Most of Michelle's friends and schoolmates were Jewish, and her family belonged to the local Reform temple, where she attended Hebrew school twice a week. "Hebrew school was a great place to hang out and have fun with Jewish friends," she recalls. "I learned the Hebrew alphabet, songs, the *Shema*, and Jewish history and identity. I felt happy being Jewish."

As she approached her teens, Michelle felt she should focus on one of her many activities and truly excel. "My major interest competing with dance was diving," she says. "But it was getting scary. While practicing a dive off the three-meter board, I smacked my back on the water and had the wind knocked out of me. At another practice a few months later, I broke my nose. I was also about to move up an age group, which meant learning very difficult dives. That was partly why I ultimately went with dance instead of diving. But as time went by, I realized that my choice was *bashert*. As an art form, dance gave me so much more than a sport ever could. It gave me a way to express myself."

Michelle began dancing far more hours a week and attending a wider variety of classes. At age 14, she joined the Fort Lauderdale Children's Ballet Theater. She flourished there, honored with solos and principal roles.

At the end of middle school, Michelle chose a private high school that happened to be Roman Catholic. It was her first time in a completely non-Jewish environment. Her new curriculum included a daily Catholic theology class, and she was expected to attend mass regularly. But she didn't mind. "To be honest, I didn't feel so different from anyone else," she admits. "Theology was just a class like any other, and I found it interesting to learn about another religion. Plus it was fun being one of the only Jews around, because I got to answer—rightly or wrongly—everyone's questions about Judaism."

Throughout high school, dancing dominated Michelle's life. Despite all her progress, however, she soon faced a disheartening reality. "At auditions, I saw how great the other dancers were," she relates. "I slowly realized that, even if I was decent in my little corner of the world, there was a huge world beyond it in which I didn't even rate. While I got into some summer programs—none of them top-tier—I was rejected from many others. When I decided to attend the Virginia School of the Arts one summer, I was put into a lower level than all my friends. It was so disappointing."

But Michelle didn't give up. "Rejection made me push harder and improve my skills to the best of my ability," she says. "I focused on building technique." By the next summer, she had caught up with her peers.

In Michelle's senior year, an event shook her comfortable, sheltered suburban existence: She went to Poland with March of the Living, a Holocaust education program. She came back profoundly changed.

"All the things about my school that I previously hadn't cared about—the Catholic students, the Catholic education, the Catholic environment—started really bothering me," she remembers. "For the first time, I sensed I didn't fit in. The difference between the other students and me, which once felt superficial, now felt deeper, but I couldn't put my finger on why. Maybe something had opened up in me Jewishly, but it was still pretty hidden. All I knew was that I couldn't go to mass anymore, or to my theology class. And it wasn't just the religion issue. My friends were all excited about the prom, but I wasn't into it. How could I get excit-ed about something that seemed so trivial in comparison to what I had seen and experienced? No one could understand what I was going through or why I was so shaken."

Michelle graduated high school as a National Merit Scholar and went off to Northwestern University in Chica-go, majoring in dance along with human development and psychological services. Knowing she wasn't cut out to be a ballerina, she found her place in modern dance.

"I was so happy to discover I could excel in an area of dance that fit my body type and ability," Michelle reflects. "Unlike other styles, the modern dance I studied was more free-form. It's about release within the structure and more nuanced choices for the entire body system. Instead of trav-eling the same pathways over and over in different combina-tions, it's about finding new ones.

"Modern dance can be weird. It's often not traditionally 'beautiful.' It's sometimes bizarre and quirky. There's a lot of artistic license. But in that world, I found my niche."

Whatever her Poland trip might have opened up Jew-ishly, Michelle didn't seek out any Jewish activities on cam-pus. Sophomore year, however, she began dating Andrew, accompanying him to the Shabbat dinners sponsored by the Meor outreach organization. "I totally wasn't into Judaism, but Andrew was becoming intellectually engaged," Michelle recounts. "He was having all these arguments with the cam-pus rabbi, trying to convince him that he was wrong about Torah and Orthodoxy. After endless debates, he had to ad-mit that the rabbi might be right. I discouraged his interest."

When Andrew, two years her senior, graduated and moved to the East Coast, they broke up.

In her junior year, Michelle interned with a local dance company. In addition to dancing, she learned about arts administration and company management. Unbeknownst to her, this training would prove invaluable.

In Michelle's senior year, her long dormant, barely-sensed spirituality finally bubbled to the surface: She discovered Judaism.

"I was working at one of the best dance companies in the world," she relates. "Its members were living every young dancer's dream—but they weren't happy. I realized that if *they* weren't happy, there was no hope for the rest of us! The whole time I worked there—nearly a year—I kept mulling this over."

Michelle decided she needed a break. She signed up for Meor's two-week study trip to Israel. It changed her life.

"The classes really spoke to me," Michelle recounts. "Each day I heard a new idea or concept in Judaism that made so much sense. I thought, 'Wow—living with this principle in mind could add so much to my life!' The one that hit home most was that everyone had a unique, God-given potential and role to fulfill in this world. With all the struggles of self-esteem among women on campus, this insight truly moved me."

When she came back from Israel, she called Andrew. "I apologized for having been so negative about Judaism, because clearly there was real beauty in it that I could see only now."

Michelle started becoming observant. She began attending Meor classes, but her dance schedule often interfered.

Fortunately, she more than made up for whatever she missed in the classroom by spending time in the nearby Jewish community of West Rogers Park. "I was there every Shabbos I wasn't performing," Michelle recounts. "The families were amazing. They took me in as if I were one of their own."

As she grew in observance, Michelle faced a formidable obstacle. Many of her dance rehearsals and performances were on Saturdays, and she was now committed to being *shomer Shabbat*. Somehow she had to negotiate between her dancing and her newfound religiosity. She recalls one particular story.

"There was a choreographer whose class I had attended since my freshman year. Her style of modern dance was extremely challenging, but after studying it for so long, I started speaking her language, and I loved it. She and I also had great chemistry. So when she didn't cast me for a big performance, I was devastated. I knew it was because I couldn't rehearse on Shabbos, which meant missing half the rehearsals. It was tempting to try and find a way to participate in those rehearsals, but instead of compromising my beliefs, I stood firm. I e-mailed her that while I was very disappointed, I understood.

"A half hour later, she asked to meet with me. The director of the dance program was also there. They let me be in the piece and share the role with another student who would take my place at Saturday rehearsals, and I would catch up on Sundays. This had never been done before! I was so grateful to be able to dance in her work without giving up on my religious principles!"

In 2011, Michelle graduated *summa cum laude* and left for Israel to study Torah at Neve Yerushalayim. She loved the learning and blossomed religiously. In Jerusalem, however, she encountered more than just Torah. "To my surprise, I met *frum* women—some quite a bit older than me, but much like myself—who loved dance, understood the importance of good training, and were amazing dancers," she says. "It was so wonderful dancing with other *frum* women!" Neve let her cut classes one or two mornings a week to go to attend dance classes with them, some of whom became her mentors.

But Michelle needed more. "After my last dance performance at Northwestern, I'd cried and cried," Michelle recounts. "I loved performing and didn't know when I'd ever get the chance again. But my campus *rebbetzin* told me that if I wanted to dance in the Jewish world, I would undoubtedly create opportunities to do so."

Remembering these words, Michelle and another former dance major choreographed a piece and performed it along with a few other students at a school event. The audience loved it and even demanded an encore.

On the heels of their success, the Neve administration asked Michelle if she'd perform the work at their community-wide Chanukah celebration, which drew more than 1,000 women. There was just one caveat. "Although the song we'd used was *frum*, they told us it wouldn't be appropriate for this more conservative audience," Michelle relates. "They asked if we could change it. 'I'm sorry,' I told them, 'but I'm an artist. We choreographed it to this specific song.' I felt very strongly about this and refused to budge.

"Then a very special *madrichah* spoke with me. 'Michelle,' she said, 'you're being selfish. Hashem has given you a gift. If you could figure out a way to dance for this audience, do you know how many women you could inspire? But you won't even try!' That really made me think. I realized she was right. So I looked for another song. I found a very interesting instrumental number that felt totally different. I tried the choreography with it, and guess what? I liked the way the quality of movement changed. It became a completely different piece. I even preferred it to the original! So we performed it for the event. Thank God, that *madrichah* opened my eyes to the possibilities of using my dance in the *frum* world."

From that incident, the Neve Dance Company was born. Michelle and her dancers were soon asked to perform in several other shows around Jerusalem, including one called *Reach for the Stars* at the Great Synagogue. Michelle had found her niche—and had learned the value of being not only an artist, but a giver.

That February, Andrew reentered Michelle's life. He'd been working in his dream job and living his dream life, but something was missing. So he'd taken the plunge and come to study in Jerusalem. Sometime later, he heard that Michelle had chosen the same path. They resumed their relationship, and in June they were married.

The newlyweds spent their first year of marriage in Jerusalem. Michelle continued at Neve while growing her dance company. During the next two years, the troupe performed and inspired over 2,000 women with their unique blend of dance and Torah.

In the summer of 2013, expecting their first child, Michelle and her husband returned to the U.S. They settled in Silver Spring, Maryland, where she began attending dance classes. "I met some people in the Jewish community, but I still felt alone," Michelle recalls. "I was constantly running out to dance with and be around people who spoke my dance 'language' and took me seriously. I would dress with *tznius* and cover my hair. Even after I had my baby, I brought him to class. It was so refreshing to be able to express the part of myself that needed to dance."

Many mothers in Michelle's neighborhood asked if she would give dance classes for their daughters. "I suspected that these moms just wanted a fun movement outlet for their girls, like Zumba," Michelle says. "I wasn't interested in that limited range. Dance is so much more to me."

But then Michelle recalled the *madrichah* telling her it was selfish not to share her gift. She also realized that teaching dance the way she wanted would fill a deep personal, spiritual need—and again, she remembered her *rebbetzin*'s words about creating opportunities. "I wanted to give of myself and the abilities Hashem gave me in a meaningful way," she states. "I wanted to be whole—to unite the dancer in me with my Jewish *neshamah*.

"I realized I could dance while giving the gift of dance to other religious girls. Even if only a few *frum* girls would benefit and find their 'thing,' their place to call home, it would be worth it."

So Michelle decided to start a dance class. But because there were different age groups, she needed at least two classes. Some girls wanted different styles, so she opened a third. Then a fourth. "Before I knew it, I was starting a real business. My husband came up with the name: La Zooz ['To Move' in Hebrew]."

La Zooz opened in January 2015. The first 45 students, ages 3 to 18, studied ballet and jazz. The girls loved it. But some parents had issues.

"I got a ton of flack," Michelle recalls. "My vision of a *frum* dance school was very different from other people's. I wanted to teach skills, develop technique, and show my students what they were capable of. People warned me that such a serious program wouldn't succeed in my community. They said I'd have to scale down my ambitions. But I wouldn't.

"Then there was the end-of-year performance. I felt very strongly that there should be a big, beautiful, professional show with real costumes and lighting. To cover expenses, I charged an additional $50 performance fee—relatively little compared to most dance schools. Parents objected. 'People here don't have that kind of money,' they said. 'Our girls are totally fine doing something simple in the school gym.' I calmly replied that the performance was an extremely important learning tool. A small-scale show wouldn't impart the value of investing so much time and energy in developing a real skill set. Just as davening in a beautiful place inspires *kavanah*, I told these mothers, performing in a special setting will inspire your daughters to work hard to match the venue. But people still discouraged me."

These conversations left Michelle frustrated. "It was awful," she confessed. "I felt so defeated. I would vent to my husband that they didn't understand what I was trying to accomplish and that maybe I should just give in and give them what they wanted. I even considered two tracks: one for girls who were serious about dance and one for those who just wanted to have fun. But Andrew convinced me to hold on to my vision, to remain true to my ideal and the unique program I had to offer."

That first year culminated in a professional performance at the American Dance Institute. Over 100 women attended—and they were impressed. "After the mothers got a taste of what was possible and what I was trying to do with these girls, I saw a major shift in perspective," Michelle reports. La Zooz had arrived.

The following year, Michelle opened a professional studio at the Yeshiva of Greater Washington girls' school, complete with a proper floor, mirrors, and barres. In December 2016, she produced a major performance featuring not only adult dancers but musicians and vocalists from the community.

By the 2018–19 school year, La Zooz was providing 16 classes a week for over 120 students in preschool through 12th grade, with more than a dozen girls taking classes twice a week. The Yeshiva of Greater Washington allowed the use of another room as a second dance studio, and Michelle rented the social hall of a new synagogue to accommodate additional classes. La Zooz had taken root and become an established and appreciated part of the Silver Spring community.

"I've weeded out the girls who just want to bounce around on stage in a pretty tutu," she explains. "That's fine, but it's not what we do in La Zooz. Real dance is hard and you have to work at it. My students are committed to building their skills. They see their progress and how much they're attaining."

After several years in the community, Michelle better understands most families' finances and now charges a modest
costume rental fee of $25. "I spend dozens of hours looking
for costumes that fit our budget and our *tznius* guidelines,"
she says. "I've learned how to shop clearance costume sites
and reuse costumes from previous years, changing things
around to make them new."

Michelle sees dance as a way to develop much more than
just dancing skills. "Dance promotes self-awareness and a
healthy body image," she notes. "It inspires self-expression,
encourages creativity, and develops discipline. It teaches life
skills, such as focus and perseverance, which can be applied
to davening and schoolwork. It may be a fun after-school activity, but it's so much more. Dance can truly change a girl's
life."

The students who've stuck with it love her approach, and adults are enthusiastic. "The first-grade class choreographed their own *siddur*-party dance," Michelle relates. "Their teachers commented that the girls clearly were getting good training and using it in a beautiful way."

Indeed, Michelle reports that most of the community has totally come around. "*Baruch Hashem*, now almost everyone gets why serious dance study is so important," she says. "People support it and are thrilled that it's available to their girls." She has also spoken in many communities about her story and her dance school.

Although La Zooz has been wildly popular, Michelle has had detractors. "One mother with a very strong personality called me the first year," she recounts. "She argued that I was missing out on a whole population by performing for women only. She wanted her husband to be in the audience as well, claiming that since the girls in her daughter's class were only in first grade, it wasn't a problem halachically. She insisted that, minimally, when her husband picked up her daughter from the class, he should be able to go in and see her dancing. 'After all,' she said, 'he's paying for it!'

"She left me feeling confused and somewhat helpless. So I said he could come in for the last five minutes of class. When he did, one girl felt so uncomfortable, she hid under a table. At that moment, I knew I had to trust my instincts and stand up for what I believed. This program had to be geared toward girls who couldn't go anywhere else due to their sensitivities, whereas the 'whole population' I was supposedly missing out on could dance at any other studio."

Michelle explained all this to the mother, who understood and gave in.

Since then, all the feedback has been highly positive. Post-performance e-mails from mothers have included comments such as "Thank you for giving the girls of our community a place to shine and develop their talents and gifts!" and "Thanks for giving all these precious girls an incredible opportunity!"

The girls themselves have expressed how much dance means to them. "In sixth grade, everyone was asked to write a persuasive essay, and several of my students wrote about why the school should offer dance as an alternative to physical education," Michelle says, smiling. In the annual literary journal, one girl described her feelings about her dance classes: "I feel accomplished. I am a fairy with gentle, waving wings, flying above the clouds, spreading my magic. [...] My teacher continues to singsong the instructions for this dance, but I am somewhere else, on top of the world." Another penned a near haiku: "Gracefully leaping / Feet flashing across the floor / Dancing is my passion."

"Many students have begged me to run a dance camp or teach during the summer," Michelle reports. "But I need a break!" Meanwhile, as her students improve, she keeps upgrading her classes, so they can continue developing as dancers.

Michelle credits her ability to be "out of the box" to her tremendously supportive husband. "With every hurdle, every painful e-mail or comment, he was there building me up," she says. "Now that I've earned a place as a respected contributor of something special in this community, I handle criticism much better and can more easily give myself the pep talks I need. But I don't know how I would have gotten my program off the ground without Andrew reminding me I was making a difference."

La Zooz has benefitted not only her students, but Michelle herself. "Running La Zooz has changed my life," she says. "Before I found an outlet for my abilities, I felt so alone. I felt I was hiding a part of myself that was dying to burst forth. *Baruch Hashem*, I've found the right avenue for it. I've also come to love teaching and engaging with these highly motivated students. I come back from class energized and inspired."

I asked Michelle to describe what dancing itself does for her. "There are no words for it," she replied. "It's a feeling of flying, of all your creative energy being focused on one place. When I dance, I'm not thinking about anything else. It's all about the movement, the expression, the music, the building and releasing of energy and momentum. It's effortless, energizing, ethereal, and other-worldly."

As a dancer, has Michelle sacrificed by leaving the secular world? "Out there, I would be one in thousands upon thousands of dancers looking to live their dream and perform. Today, with the influx of highly skilled, well-trained *ba'alot teshuvah*, there's much more room for self-expression in all-female environments, and there are so many opportunities to perform and connect with other talented artists. I've made a difference in the *frum* world that I would never have made in the larger, secular world. I've found a niche for myself and my craft, and I'm so grateful that I chose this path.

"As a religious artist, I'm serving the Creator through something I love so much. Inspiring through movement.

Engaging young minds. Developing self-esteem. Helping girls build a skill from the ground up. To take your art and make it meaningful—who could ask for more?"

According to the Sages (Exodus Rabbah 29:1), God "speaks" to every person according to his or her unique strength, and how you "hear" a mitzvah depends upon your prism of experience: your upbringing, life circumstances, personality, and more. Therefore, only you can do a mitzvah the way you do—and every time you do, something new comes into the world. (Gilla Rosen)

Chapter Six
Caring for Creation

WALKING DOWN THE street one day, I passed a parked truck as its driver thoughtlessly tossed an empty yogurt container out the window and onto the sidewalk.

I picked up his garbage and walked over to him. "Why?" I asked in Hebrew. "This is Jerusalem, God's holy city, and we dump trash on it?" "You're right," he said sheepishly as I dropped the container in a nearby bin.

The truth is, *all* the earth is God's (not just Jerusalem). But do we treat it accordingly?

For Naomi Elbinger, born in 1978, caring for the earth is as much a part of her as breathing. It all began when, as a child, she saw a picture of a dead seal. Its head had gotten stuck in the plastic packaging of a six-pack, and it had choked to death. "That photo really shook me," she recalls. "I couldn't get the image out of my head. Someone was having fun at the beach and just tossed away a six-pack holder.

An innocent act, but it caused something so awful and ugly. That was an awakening."

Naomi grew up in Sydney, where nature is widely appreciated. An avid hiker and camper, she developed a passion for the environment, even digging up her parents' lawn to create a vegetable garden.

Naomi was a deep-thinking, inquisitive child. Things had to make sense to her. Her Jewish upbringing didn't. While her parents were committed, practicing Jews, they lacked the education to back up their beliefs. She knew her own Judaism required a more solid foundation.

It's no coincidence that Naomi's spiritual awakening came through marveling at God's creation. When she was 21 and studying in Thailand, the transformative moment occurred:

"One night I joined a bunch of friends going to town. On the way, I glanced up at the night sky and saw it was filled with the most brilliant stars. I begged my friends to lie down on the grass and stargaze with me. They reluctantly agreed. We lay there for about five minutes, and I felt transported by the awesome breadth of the star-studded heavens. My friends were growing impatient, however, so we moved on.

"In town, there was music and food and drink. Everything was loud and brash, filthy and packed, smoky and seedy. People were having a great time. But I just wanted to go back to the stars.

"I vowed never again to attend a party unless there was something truly worth celebrating, and unless I could keep my eye on the stars—meaning what I truly cared about. After that night I made some big, difficult changes, which led me to the lifestyle I lead today."

Back in Sydney, Naomi started going to Torah class-es and reading Jewish books. About a year later, she made *aliyah*. In Israel, Naomi continued to grow in observance. Within two years, she met her husband-to-be, Shmuel Yo-sef. By then, Naomi was deeply religious. "Judaism provides many opportunities to celebrate," she says, "without ever los-ing sight of the stars."

The couple settled in Jerusalem. Naomi's new neighbor-hood provided the religious environment she had lacked in Sydney. But the physical environment was a different story. "Garbage was everywhere," she reports. "Scenic spots weren't treasured or even conserved. There was this alienation from the environment. It was astounding. And a shame, because appreciating the wonder and beauty of creation is a great way to connect to Hashem." While many of her neighbors sympathized with her concerns, people seemed too busy to do anything about them.

This situation bothered Naomi deeply. But what could one person do? For years she despaired of change and re-signed herself to the status quo.

Finally, in 2016, she'd had enough. It was time to take action. A friend introduced her to an idealistic Israeli named Avishai Himmelfarb. Himmelfarb had started an organiza-tion called Leshomra, taken from God's command to Adam: "God took the man and placed him in the Garden of Eden, to work it and *to guard it* [*leshomra*]" (Genesis 2:15). Leshom-ra's educational farm tours inspired people to love and care for God's creation. Himmelfarb had also recently developed a Torah-based school program to teach religious children about nature, environmental responsibility, agriculture, and love of the Land of Israel. He sorely needed help getting his initiative off the ground.

Naomi checked out the curriculum. The first lesson featured a photo of a suffocated sea turtle, a discarded plastic wrapper stuck in its throat. She'd found her calling.

A keen businesswoman and entrepreneur, Naomi was skilled in marketing, grant writing, website design, and public relations. She'd been one of the main organizers of the Temech Conference, the world's first and largest business meeting for religious Jewish women. Most important, she was passionate enough about the environment to get involved. She could make Leshomra everything it could be.

With Naomi as volunteer deputy director, Leshomra took off. It started in the city of Modi'in Illit (in central Israel), whose municipality generously assisted financially. "The response was incredible," Naomi recounts. "Everyone saw the need for the program and was so enthusiastic about it. They loved it right away."

Leshomra then expanded to Jerusalem. Funding was offered for a pilot program in 20 preschools, but after seeing what Leshomra was about, 60 applied. "The teachers had never been exposed to this approach," Naomi says. "They were all so touched by it and excited about bringing it to their students."

Leshomra has spread to 121 locations all over Israel, plus one in Manchester. Some 180 teachers have been trained by Leshomra, and 20 Bais Yaakov graduates have been certified as ecology guides. After-school gardening and nature activities have been launched in community centers, and over 7,000 youngsters and their parents have participated in farm tours.

Leshomra's most important work takes place in the classroom. Children learn about local fauna, water conservation, soil, and the environmental damage caused by littering. They recycle, build birdhouses, and plant and harvest their own vegetables.

"Leshomra has changed kids' lives," Naomi states. "They needed to get their hands dirty, to learn about wildlife, to watch things grow. They needed to be in touch with nature. And we've gotten amazing feedback from parents. They say the program has captivated kids who were withdrawn, have ADHD, or simply learn differently."

Adults in Naomi's community who haven't been exposed to Leshomra aren't always as enthusiastic as teachers, children, and parents who have. "While there's no opposition," she says, "not everyone understands why Leshomra is so valuable. A few regard it as bizarre or a waste of time. Others are just apathetic."

Naomi humorously describes an experience she's had more than once:

At a community event, I start chatting with one of the women.

"What do you do?" she asks.

"I volunteer for a non-profit that's bringing farming and other nature experiences to a *cheder* and Bais Yaakov near you!"

"Oh… [awkward pause]. I wonder who made these brownies. They're so good. I think I'll get another one."

Frequent encounters with people who don't appreciate Naomi's work can wear her down. "I'll start to question why I'm investing in a project whose payoff is subtle and largely in the future, when I could be raising money for poor brides or organizing meals for women after birth—more typical *chesed* projects with immediate benefits and greater respect."

The answer: It's clear to Naomi that protecting God's world is what God wants her to do.

"Most religious Jews understand the beauty of nature as a gift from Hashem, but few ask, 'So is it okay that I'm destroying it?' Because we *are* destroying it.

"Hashem has imbued me with a passion for preserving the world's beauty and nurturing the Jewish people's connection to it. Estrangement from nature causes a lot of problems, some huge. I can't solve them singlehandedly, but I can at least do my part. I couldn't live with myself if I didn't."

Naomi admits that championing an unusual cause has its emotional challenges. "Being different can be lonely," she says. "There's no glamour or glory in what I'm doing. But this is obviously part of my mission in life, so it's comforting that I'm pursuing my God-given destiny."

Over time, Leshomra has needed Naomi less, but her passion for its message has only grown. She recently began turning her humble apartment and yard into a model sustainable microfarm, giving workshops on growing and processing foods, creating all-natural household necessities, and making the most of Hashem's creation. Her neighbors are curious—and sometimes nervous—about her adventures, but she encourages them to get up close and try microfarming themselves. She's even written about urban gardening and beekeeping for *Mishpacha* magazine, generating tremendous feedback. Naomi hasn't given up the business she runs to support her family, but she's finding new and exciting ways of achieving her mission by inspiring others daily.

Naomi sees Torah and nature as deeply intertwined. "Hashem created a world in which everything is ultimately good and useful. When people eat apples, for example, they often discard the peels—they just want the 'good part.' But those peels are just as good: I use them to make cider vinegar, feed my pet chickens, or enrich the soil in my vegetable garden. The deep satisfaction you get from making the most of everything God gives you, even the 'garbage,' is hard to describe until you've experienced it.

"Nature communicates the truth that nothing is a waste, nothing a mistake. Throwing away whatever we think we don't need not only obscures that message, it deprives us of so many enriching experiences. Just as manure makes things grow, so do our challenges. Partnering with nature allows us to reflect on and tune in to the Divine in the world, which inspires awe.

"This is what I try and share with others."

Thanks to Leshomra and Naomi's new endeavors, more and more people are connecting to the wonders of nature and learning to protect them. As Naomi says, "Guarding the earth can only bring wholeness and healing to society."

> The Sages state that any fish that can't swim against the current isn't from a kosher species. This suggests that a pure person is someone who bucks the trend when necessary. (Rabbi Elimelech Biderman)

Chapter Seven

Power, Peace, Purpose

THE VOICES BOUNCE off the walls: "Power! Peace! Purpose!" It sounds like the chant of a movement. And it is—a movement of children who are learning to face a frightening disease without fear. These young martial artists are literally "kicking cancer"—thanks to one very dedicated man.

Kids Kicking Cancer is the brainchild of Rabbi Elimelech Goldberg. Born in 1956 to Orthodox Jewish parents with strong values, Rabbi Goldberg received his rabbinic ordination and graduate training in psychology from Yeshiva University. After marrying, he taught at Yeshiva University of Los Angeles. Ordinary enough. But Rabbi Goldberg is no ordinary rabbi.

The Goldberg's first child, Sara Basya, born in 1979, was diagnosed with leukemia one week before her first birthday.

She died two weeks after her second. "She was an incredibly special soul," her father remembers. "After being held down for particularly painful procedures, she'd kiss the doctors. She'd tell the five-year-olds in the clinic not to cry. And even as she suffered, she'd pat me on the shoulder and say, 'It's okay, Abba. I love you.'"

Eight years later, Rabbi Goldberg was serving as rabbi of the Young Israel of Southfield, Michigan, and maintaining a full counseling schedule. In addition, after years of study, he'd received his first black belt in Choi Kwang-Do. Unbeknownst to him, these skills would soon be used in a whole new way.

It all began with a phone call. Rabbi Simcha Scholar was soliciting donations for one of the first pediatric oncology summer camps, located in New York State. Knowing what children with cancer and their families go through, Rabbi Goldberg was more than happy to write a check and suggest other potential donors. But Rabbi Scholar wanted Rabbi Goldberg to direct the camp.

"No way," Rabbi Goldberg told him. "Every little girl there will remind me of my daughter." But Rabbi Scholar persisted. "It's not all pain and sadness," he assured Rabbi Goldberg. "It's easy to make children laugh, and when they do, they're just ordinary kids again." After serious consideration and discussion with his wife, Rabbi Goldberg became director of Camp Simcha—for 12 years.

At the camp, Rabbi Goldberg—or Rabbi G., as he affectionately came to be known—discovered a disturbing reality. "If an adult screams during an excruciating medical procedure, the doctors will usually stop and try to find another way to do it," he says. "But if children scream, the medical team often holds them down even more. As a result, these young patients feel not only fear and pain, but disempowerment."

Rabbi G. recalls how he realized he could use martial arts to help children deal with these feelings. Walking into Camp Simcha's chemotherapy room one day, he witnessed 5-year-old Josh violently resisting two nurses' attempts to hold him down for an injection. The boy was hysterical. The rabbi describes what happened next:

"I suddenly heard myself shout, 'Wait!' Everyone in the room stopped struggling at once. Even Josh stopped screaming. They all looked at me. I had no clue what to say. 'Give me five minutes with this boy,' I heard myself request. The nurses were happy to leave. Josh looked at me with relief and gratitude, as if I had just stayed his execution. I walked over to him and said, 'I'm a black belt. Do you want me to teach you some karate?' He almost jumped off the table in excitement.

"'In martial arts,' I began, 'we say that pain is a message you don't have to listen to. You can take a deep breath and push out the pain.' Five minutes later, we were doing a simple Tai Chi breathing technique together. Twenty minutes after that, a nurse removed the needle from his chest. Josh looked up at her. 'Did you do it yet?' he asked.

"At that moment, Kids Kicking Cancer was born."

In 1999, Rabbi G. launched the program that had been brewing in his mind for several years. He started with 10 children at Children's Hospital of Michigan, teaching them basic martial arts. By 2002, Kids Kicking Cancer had become a full-time job. "Although a lot of people change jobs in mid-life, the journey from Orthodox rabbi to *sensei* [martial arts teacher] is not that common," he admits. Neither is teaching karate in pediatric oncology wards, particularly as a bearded man wearing a black *kippah*.

According to Rabbi G., martial arts is much more than kicking, punching, and felling your opponent.

"Martial arts emphasize the melding of mind, body, and spirit in a fascinating amalgam of self-awareness, introspection, movement, and especially energy," he explains. "Whether one calls this energy *chi, ki, tenaga dalam, prana,* or *neshamah,* light, or soul, the theme is the same, and it mirrors Jewish mysticism. Each of us contains a power that can improve our lives and those around us."

The first step in activating this force is optimism. "Optimism enables you to take control over your life," Rabbi G. asserts. "Optimism doesn't mean everything will be great. It means you can respond to everything with greatness. We teach children to reframe their challenges as growth opportunities that can define their purpose in life and their very being."

Breath and relaxation are the core of Rabbi G.'s approach. "The Hebrew word for breath, *neshimah,* derives from the same root as *neshamah,* soul," he points out. "In Kabbalah, proper breathing and relaxation can connect you to enormous spheres of power and well-being. We teach kids to use the power of their inner light."

"Breathe in," an instructor will tell his students. "Imagine the air coming in as a beautiful and powerful light flooding your body. Then blow out all the anger, fear, and darkness, relaxing every muscle." Anger is number one. "In martial arts, anger is an enemy we must defeat before any other," Rabbi G. says. By breathing out all their negative emotions—including fear—and visualizing their inner strength, kids enter a calm, positive headspace. Then they can conquer their pain.

Kids Kicking Cancer also trains experienced martial artists to be therapists. Together with Rabbi G., they draw on dozens of different fighting styles, designing the most effective moves for his clientele. "Movement is essential for these children," Rabbi G. says. "It empowers them. In striking their tar-

get, they symbolically defeat their own internal enemy, be it fear, pain, or anger. It's also empowering to walk down a hall not just dragging an intravenous pole, but doing karate stances." And because kids know moving requires energy, they're more likely to eat despite loss of appetite.

Even more important, Kids Kicking Cancer uses meditation techniques to show youngsters how to cope with painful procedures, even working at home with children too sick to come to class.

Initially, people were skeptical about Rabbi G.'s work. "Many of my medical colleagues suggested downplaying the breath work, because it seemed beyond the pale of evidence-based medicine," Rabbi G. recounts. "In other words, they thought it was off the wall." Fortunately, his *rosh kollel* was very supportive, as was his family. As the years went by, more and more research corroborated what he was doing.

"Brain scanning has clarified the chemical connection between stress, fear, anger, and pain," Rabbi G. reports. "People who are stressed, fearful, and angry feel greater pain. It's that simple. Proper relaxation, focus, and especially breathing reduce these feelings. Today, every U.S. hospital I visit has a breathing specialist, because this work has proven effective. Parents, doctors, nurses, and many others have been mesmerized by the changes they've seen in the children who've joined our classes."

Children are given tools they can master quickly and use wherever and whenever they're challenged. One is the "Breath Brake," using deep breathing to stretch the body upward, then gently let it fall, thereby calming it. Another is the body scan, gradually relaxing every muscle from head to toe. Kids thus surmount suffering and create their own inner peace.

Five-year-old Luca is proof. A Kids Kicking Cancer student from age 3, he once had to undergo a painful bandage removal. The nurse was about to call for someone to hold him down, but Luca told her there was no need. "I'm a martial artist," he said. "I'll teach you how to do our power breathing." He then breathed out the pain. Even as his skin tore, he remained totally calm. "I've been in nursing for ages," the nurse told his mother, "but I've never seen anything like this."

Finding meaning in adversity helps us overcome it. That's why Rabbi G. also gives his youngsters a strong sense of purpose.

"Our kids are taught that their mission is to share what they've learned in order to help others cope with their own difficulties," he says. "These children have actually taught adults with cancer and other serious illnesses. They've even instructed military personnel in using breathing to alleviate combat stress and trauma. The more purpose they feel, the less pain they experience."

Rabbi G. makes sure that the kids know how much they're benefitting others. When a graduate student named Nicole told him she fainted at the sight of needles, Rabbi G. taught her a meditation his student Desi had used to conquer significant pain, adding that if it worked, she should let the girl know. It did, and Nicole immediately contacted her. "I'm so happy I no longer have this fear in my life!" she wrote. "The whole time I was thinking of you and how brave you are. Desi, you changed my life!" Desi's mother later reported that she was walking around the house saying, "I can't believe it—I really am powerful!"

Power, peace, purpose. It works. A study published in *The Journal of Pediatric Health, Medicine and Therapeutics* found that over 85% of Rabbi G.'s kids reported a lessening of their pain, with an average reduction of 40%. "Children who've been given a difficult diagnosis can feel like victims," says Rabbi G. "We help them see themselves as victors."

Every participant in Kids Kicking Cancer becomes part of its "Heroes' Circle." "Separating our souls from cancer and its challenges liberates us," Rabbi G. affirms. "That's called living heroically."

Tragically, not all these heroes respond to treatment. Kids Kicking Cancer's "black belt" program teaches them that while they may succumb to cancer physically, they needn't succumb spiritually. During a child's last days, he or she receives a black belt in a public ceremony. Embroidered on the belt are the words "Master Teacher," in recognition of his or her spiritual triumph in teaching the world how to use the power of light to break through darkness.

Brendan was one such child. At age 9, after battling cancer for four years, he had to be carried on stage in his karate uniform to collect his black belt. Brendan was too weak even to speak, so Rabbi G. read his acceptance speech to the crowd. "I am receiving this black belt because I have defeated my cancer," he wanted his audience to know. "I'm no longer afraid or angry. If anything, I'm more connected to God and the people around me." Amid a standing ovation, Brendan drew on every last ounce of strength he had to rise, wearing his new black belt.

"That moment was a celebration of victory, of life, and ultimately of a light that is forever," Rabbi G. says. "A little boy standing up changed the lives of 300 people."

A week later, Brendan was buried in his black belt. People often ask Rabbi G. how he deals with children's deaths. "I cry," he replies simply. "For me, however, the greatest tragedy isn't the death of a child, it's the loss of someone who never understood what life is all about.

"Too many of our children have short lives, but they have long days. Because they're so young, their lives are all the more profound. The triumph of a soul that finds meaning and strength within trauma impacts the entire world, especially when that soul is a child."

In 2004, Rabbi Goldberg traveled to Washington, D.C. to receive the nation's highest public health honor, the Robert Wood Johnson Community Health Leaders Award. That same year, he accepted the Humanitarian of the Year Award from the McCarty Cancer Foundation.

Since then, his program has branched out to Canada, Italy, Israel, and South Africa, and to children suffering from any painful illness, not just cancer. (One spin-off has been Kids Kicking Sickle Cell, as sickle cell anemia presents many of the same challenges as cancer.) Rabbi G. and his team provide sibling support, counseling, family events, and more. Their organization operates in over fifty-six hospitals and locations around the world—all free of change.

In addition to running Kids Kicking Cancer, Rabbi Goldberg is a clinical assistant professor of pediatrics at Wayne State University School of Medicine, where he teaches the science of stress and pain management. He also conducts stress seminars at Fortune 500 companies and lectures worldwide on spirituality and health.

As a black belt martial arts instructor and teacher of breathing and meditation, how does Rabbi G. stay "out of the box" while remaining part of the mainstream Orthodox community? "I just redefine the box," he says, "and then explain how we all can use it." In other words, something new and different becomes accepted when people see the good it's doing. "Actually," Rabbi G. adds, "there's no such thing as a box. We each have our own pathway to Hashem, to actualizing our potential by spreading His light."

By reflecting the Divine light through his own unique prism, Rabbi Elimelech Goldberg has helped countless children do the same.*

> Why doesn't the Torah describe the second day of creation as "good" (like all the other days)? One biblical commentary, the Kli Yakar, explains that nothing new was created that day. Goodness lies in originality and innovation. (Rabbi Mattisyahu Solomon)

---

* Parts of this chapter were adapted from Rabbi Goldberg's book, *A Perfect God Created an Imperfect World Perfectly: 30 Life Lessons from Kids Kicking Cancer.*

Chapter Eight

Putting Women Back in the Picture

IT'S AN IMAGE the world has never forgotten. In June 1985, the cover of *National Geographic* featured a 12-year-old Afghani girl who had fled the invading Soviets and was living in a refugee camp in Pakistan. Wearing a torn, rust-colored dress and headscarf, she stared at the camera, her large, piercing green eyes resembling those of a hunted animal. The girl immediately became an emblem for refugees the world over. "People volunteered to work in the refugee camps because of that photo," remarked Steve McCurry, who took the picture. "It drew attention to [the refugees'] plight and inspired a lot of people." Years later, the National Geographic Society tracked down the girl—by then a wife and mother—and set up the Afghan Children's Fund in her honor.

All because of a picture.

Images are powerful. One photo of an emaciated baby generates more charity for starving children in Africa than reams of statistics. Numbers speak to the mind, but pictures touch the heart.

Artist Ann Koffsky understands the power of pictures. "Images are a unique way to communicate, evoke emotion, and create connection," she says. "Words are also great, but 'a picture is worth a thousand words.'" In 2012, she decided that pictures were also worth fighting for.

Born in 1972, Ann has always been an independent thinker. Although she was raised Orthodox, her father was the rabbi of a Conservative synagogue, and there were very few Jews in her neighborhood. "It was a kind of split-personality life," Ann recounts. "It definitely gave me a unique perspective."

From a young age, Ann was a gifted writer, but her first love was drawing. "Art was the primary means by which I created, expressed myself, and contributed something unique to the world," she says. "Others could produce better art, but only I could make *my* art. That gave me a sense of individuality and purpose."

Combining her artistic and literary skills, Ann became a successful author of Torah literature for kids. But in recent years, something new drew her attention.

"It kind of snuck up on me," Ann recounts. "Jewish newspapers, magazines, brochures, ads—more and more, they contained no pictures of women. It's hard to see something that isn't there, so I noticed it before my friends did.

"As a student of Jewish art history, I knew there was no halachah banning pictures of women. On the contrary, from ancient times, images of women have figured in everything from synagogue mosaics to haggadot. Yehudit, a heroine in rabbinic literature, has been sculpted on menorahs, and illuminated *Megillot Ester* certainly depict the title character. Photos of women have even appeared in Agudath Israel publications, the *Jewish Observer*, and biographies of great rabbis.

"So this new policy was completely unprecedented, and I realized its dangers. Yet whenever I brought up the subject, most people were unconcerned."

Personally, when pictures accompany an article about a woman, I get a better sense of who she is and connect to her more. According to Ann, however, the issue is much larger.

"First there's the educational aspect," she explains. "Like it or not, we live in a very visual world. When we remove pictures of religious women from the public realm, the only females left are Disney princesses or, worse, fashion models. Is that what we want? Our daughters need images of modest Jewish girls and righteous women to admire and emulate. Just as it's meaningful to gaze at pictures of great rabbis, a picture of a great Jewish woman can be equally inspiring."

Then there's the economic fallout: Not showing pictures of women can hurt those same women's ability to earn a living. For example, Facebook ads with photos generate a response rate of 80% or more, whereas ads without them average only around 10%. That's because pictures make advertisers seem more real and personable.

Ann shared an illustrative anecdote: "A public relations person from a Jewish outreach organization deleted the head shots of its women speakers from an ad so it could run in a popular magazine. I asked him, 'Why don't you omit the pictures of both men and women, so the latter aren't singled out?' He responded, 'But then the ad will be less effective.' *Exactly.*"

Furthermore, says Ann, communication about important issues is weakened when there's no photo of the spokeswoman. Stories are less impactful when unaccompanied by pictures of the female characters. And erasing women and girls simply disenfranchises them.

Finally, there's the whole issue of how women should be regarded. "Removing pictures of modestly dressed women implies that men are incapable of viewing them just as people," Ann contends. "That's demeaning not only to women, but to men themselves, who I believe deserve more credit. Men interact with women at the office, the bank, the grocery store—pretty much everywhere. Can they not be trusted to see appropriate photos of them?"

For all these reasons, Ann was frustrated by the trend she'd identified. Then she realized that, as an artist, she could contribute to people's thinking on the matter.

"I didn't know if I could change anyone's mind," Ann says. "But I was inspired by the famous Jewish saying '*lo alecha hamelachah ligmor*'—you don't have to finish the work [but neither are you free to exempt yourself from it]. Whether or not I succeeded, I had to try. I also remembered, *lehavdil*, an episode of the *West Wing* TV show. The president is considering appointing a Supreme Court justice who's likeable but unimpressive. Another character argues the importance of having a truly excellent judge, who's willing to take an unpopular stance. 'Who will write the extraordinary dissent?' that character says. 'The minority opinion whose time hasn't come, but 20 years later, some clerk digs it up and realizes its value?'

"I felt I had to write that dissent. Maybe someone would read it—if not now, then maybe 20 years from now. And my great-great-grandchildren would know that when Grandma saw something wrong, she said something."

In the fall of 2012, Ann wrote an opinion piece for *Jewish Action*. "Please Put the Women Back In" described the power of images and what's lost when women are excluded. The essay was widely read and got the ball rolling. The *Flatbush Jewish Journal* reprinted the piece, generating 10 weeks' worth of letters. More women followed Ann's lead, speaking out in other publications. A Facebook group called "Put the Women Back in Frum Media!" was formed, which Ann excitedly joined. Members organized a petition and letter-writing campaign, urging Jewish magazines, charity organizations, and even toy companies to stop eliminating females. Ann published several more articles elsewhere and began lecturing on the topic. Finally, she created a website, *frumwomenhavefaces.com*, which presents a thoughtful critique of the erasure of women, including quotes from prominent rabbis.

As the movement gained momentum, Bais Yaakov graduate Rivka Lieberman also took action. "How can I raise my daughters to be *tzanua*," she lamented, "if the publications I'm bringing into my home imply that no woman is *tzanua* enough to be seen?" So Rivka launched *Tmunah* [Picture] *Jr.*, a Jewish magazine for children featuring pictures of both males and females.

Through the Facebook group, Ann met Dr. Leslie Ginsparg Klein, academic dean of WITS/Maalot, the Women's Institute of Torah Seminary, in Baltimore. Together they came up with another way to put women back in media: They coauthored *Sarah Builds a School*, a children's book about Sarah Schenirer, founder of the Bais Yaakov movement. The pair hope this tale of female leadership—including, obviously, plenty of pictures of Sarah Schenirer—will provide young girls with a role model.

Meanwhile, due to social pressure, *Mishpacha* has added women's photos to its website and social media accounts and is including more drawings (if not photos) of women in the magazine itself. "We're not there yet," Ann says, "but it's a move in the right direction."

The women are coming back.

Of course, not everyone agrees with Ann. Many have attacked her position, feeling that not publishing pictures of women is a matter of modesty.

Pictured above: Sara Schenirer; Rishel Kotler; Margalit Yosef; Sarah'la, daughter of the Chofetz Chaim; Henny Machlis; Esther Jungreis; Ruchoma Shain; Batsheva Kanievsky; Chaya Mushka Schneerson

"I don't believe *tzniut* means being invisible," Ann counters. "It means acting appropriately and with dignity, wherever we are. It's possible to be both public and *tzanua*. It all depends on *why* we're in the public eye and how we comport ourselves while we're there.

"In the book of Ruth, the return of Ruth and Naomi to the Land of Israel is incredibly public. The text basically says the whole community stared at them. Yet the Midrash tells us that Ruth possessed the utmost *tzniut*. I think that's because she wasn't after self-promotion, fame, or glory. She entered the Land for Naomi, for Torah, and for Hashem—all causes greater than herself.

"If we want a modern-day example, we can learn from Rebbetzin Esther Jungreis (of blessed memory). Her picture often appeared in the press and graced the cover of one of her books. She even spoke at the Republican National Convention, where she was seen by millions. But why was she there? To share Hashem's Torah. And how did she act? With regal grace and dignity.

"Like these great women, we should all strive to be forces of good wherever we find ourselves. Acting dignified in public makes a *kiddush Hashem* and is the ultimate expression of *tzniut*."

Nevertheless, Ann has found herself in a whirlwind of controversy. How does she cope?

"Being an artist helps," she says. "As a student, I had to put my work on the wall and listen to everyone's critiques. And when I started writing books, I got rejected by a lot of publishers. As a result, I'm pretty thick-skinned.

"In any case, my own community is supportive, even though some are taken aback by my passion for this issue.

Thankfully, my husband and kids actually appreciate my be-ing 'out of the box.'"

Ann's great-great-grandchildren will be proud.

> A student of Rabbi Shlomo Freifeld's with little Jewish background eventually became a Torah scholar, settled in Israel, and secured a prestigious rabbinic position. When Rabbi Freifeld visited him, the young man expressed all kinds of politically correct views. "My dear friend," Rabbi Freifeld said, "you've truly come a long way. But I do miss one thing—you used to think for yourself." (Rabbi Yisroel Besser)

Chapter Nine
It All Started at the Wall

ᴊᴇʀᴜsᴀʟᴇᴍ, Dᴇᴄᴇᴍʙᴇʀ 1980. A young American tourist wearing jeans and a backpack descends the steps to the Kotel plaza. Gazing at the Wall for the first time, she knows she's supposed to be moved. But she's too annoyed—even angry—about the partition separating men and women. *Why are women shunted off to the side?* she fumes. She makes a decision. *These religious people can segregate themselves if they like, but I'm standing wherever I want.* And she marches right into the men's section.

She's about halfway to the Kotel when a guard suddenly notices her. Running after the girl, he calls to her to stop. "You not to be here, you to be *there*," he says in broken English, pointing to the women's side. He escorts her out. She's seeing red.

At that moment, a tall man wearing a suit and a black fedora approaches her. He smiles. "Are you Jewish?" he asks.

"Yes," she says, between clenched teeth.

"Would you be interested in a Friday night Shabbat meal with a religious family, or a class on Jewish philosophy?"

"No!" she replies, wanting nothing to do with either the Kotel or Judaism.

For the next few hours, she wanders around the Old City. But something pulls her back to the Kotel. *I'll give it a second chance*, she figures. Again, the partition upsets her, but she has no choice about it. On the women's side, she goes up to the Wall. Placing her hands on the stones, she sees the notes pressed into the cracks, gazes upward, and looks at the people around her, then back at the Wall. She feels nothing. *Oh well*, she thinks. *I tried*. With that, she exits the women's section.

Just then, a young woman in a high-necked sweater and mid-calf skirt approaches. "Excuse me," she says with a friendly smile, "do you have a map of the Old City?"

"Yeah, just a second," the tourist responds, reaching into her backpack.

"By the way, are you Jewish?"

Hmm, the tourist thinks. *I believe I've heard this before.* "Yes. Why?"

"While you're here in Jerusalem, would you be interested…"

Yup, sounds familiar. "Listen," the tourist challenges, "before we talk about my doing anything religious, what's the deal with this partition?"

"Well," the woman calmly replies, "wouldn't you have a hard time concentrating on your prayers if a really cute guy were standing next to you?"

The tourist pauses. *Yes, I would. Okay, that makes sense.* Then a little light bulb goes on in her head. *Maybe other things in Judaism make sense too?*

Two months later, she drops in on some classes, intending to study no longer than a week. Ten months later, she returns to America—just for a visit—as a newly Orthodox Jew.

The tourist was yours truly. The young woman was Bracha Zaret.

Born in 1958, Bracha grew up the middle child in a middle-class Jewish home in Brooklyn. Her father, a cab driver, and her mother, an assistant teacher of disabled children, both came from basically *shomer Shabbat* homes whose religious observance lacked substance. Bracha was sent to public school. "A lot was happening in America back then," she recalls. "In elementary school, girls had to wear dresses, but then came the women's movement, and by junior high we were all wearing bell-bottoms. In high school we had race riots, and the sexual revolution was going strong. Things were changing so rapidly."

Bracha, however, was more conservative than most of her peers. She was also highly outspoken. "In seventh grade, I argued with the entire class about premarital physical relationships," she recalls. "I was the only one against them." By the time Bracha was 14, and in a class for gifted students, the world was moving in one direction, but she was headed in another.

"I was introduced to Torah in Hebrew school," she recounts. "The teachers were Orthodox, and their intellectual soundness really affected me. Then I saw a David Susskind show featuring an Orthodox rabbi, and everything he said rang so true.

"But the clincher was when I met a very *frum* girl in an Orthodox day camp in the Catskills. There was something special about her. She didn't talk about religion, she just did her thing. She wore skirts, washed her hands before eating bread, and was always smiling and upbeat. Everywhere I turned, people looked unhappy, but she seemed so emotionally healthy. The disparity was glaring. I was drawn to her and what she represented."

Impressed by what she was seeing in Judaism, Bracha decided to keep Shabbat.

She joined NCSY (the National Conference of Synagogue Youth, an Orthodox outreach organization for teens) and became president of her local chapter. Even as a teenager, she brought many friends and neighbors closer to Judaism. "So much of the world was messed up, while Judaism was in tune with human nature and improved people's lives," she says. "I felt, if you found a vaccine for a terrible disease, wouldn't you want to share it? I wanted to share my Judaism."

Despite their non-observance, her parents were supportive. "There was just one time when my mother had enough," Bracha recalls. "I asked to tape the refrigerator light off for Shabbos. This 'nit-picking' sent her into a tailspin. So I dropped it and just didn't open the fridge the whole Shabbos. Eventually her 'Jewish mother' instinct—'I don't want my daughter to starve'—won out, and she let me tape the fridge light." Gradually, even deeper Jewish instincts prevailed, and Bracha's parents and younger brother also became religious.

After high school, Bracha spent two years learning Torah at Neve Yerushalayim in Jerusalem. Deeply inspired, she returned to New York to attend the Rika Breuer Teachers Seminary and then Bais Yaakov Teachers Seminary (headed by the famous Rebbetzin Vichna Kaplan, of blessed memory). She also earned a B.A. in education, then taught in the Yeshivah of Brooklyn. "I thought I would teach Torah forever," Bracha says. "I was so into it, I prepared like crazy for my classes and learned a lot in the process. Teaching also helped me develop my gift of gab." That gift proved tremendously beneficial in a very different field.

On the last day of the school year, at age 22, Bracha got engaged to Moshe, who'd been happily studying Torah in Israel. The young couple prepared to move to Jerusalem, where Moshe would continue at the Mir Yeshivah while Bracha would teach.

But God had other plans.

Reaching out to fellow Jews was in Bracha's blood. "I was friendly and outgoing, deeply committed to Judaism, and had always loved sharing what I knew with others," she says. "Even on the plane, I was inviting people for Shabbos!"

Moshe realized Bracha's talents had to be put to use. In Jerusalem, he arranged an interview for her with American P'eylim, an outreach organization that employed Rabbi Meir Schuster (of blessed memory), who famously spent his days at the Kotel connecting with Jewish tourists. P'eylim was happy to have someone join Rabbi Schuster in this unusual and demanding job.

"The Kotel was a whole little world—the guards, the beggars, and especially Rabbi Schuster," Bracha recounts.

"On Friday nights there'd be 300 people crowding around him, some students but mostly tourists, and he'd set them all up for Shabbos dinner. It was quite a scene.

"All week I'd stand at the Kotel, approaching complete strangers. It was physically taxing—especially in the summer heat—and emotionally uncomfortable, even for an extrovert like me. But I believed in what I was doing.

"The first month, I got nowhere. It was so disheartening. But my husband encouraged me. Eventually I saw results. Soon I was bringing girls to Neve or farming them out for Shabbos." Within a short time, the tireless Bracha had morphed into a female Rabbi Schuster.

Three years after introducing who knows how many people to traditional Judaism, Bracha was approached by philanthropist Barry Septimus. He was looking to donate to the cause of *kiruv*. "He asked for my wish list," Bracha says. "It was like a dream come true." Bracha envisioned outreach teams at the Hebrew University, Tel Aviv University, and all the secular Jewish institutions catering to young Jews from the States. Impressed with Bracha's energy and ambition, the benefactor consulted the renowned Rabbi Simcha Wasserman (of blessed memory), who vouched for her as well. With Septimus's backing, Bracha took her efforts to the next level.

"*Kiruv* was new then," she points out. "When I started at Hebrew U., I was pretty much the only one doing it, so I had to figure out what worked."

Bracha took a sincere interest in everyone she met. She really listened. "That's a wonderful and unfortunately rare gift to give someone, and it breaks down social barriers and creates a connection.

"Most people become religious not because of a *devar Torah*, but because they meet emotionally healthy Torah Jews. That's their window on the Jewish world. They see that *frum* people are normal and down-to-earth, happy, warm, and friendly, and genuinely want to give—such as by hosting Shabbos guests they may never see again.

"Newcomers to Judaism also learn that Orthodox Jews lead lives of personal and spiritual growth. This discovery makes people ponder the meaning of their own lives. Hopefully, they realize that the road to happiness is something different and far deeper than what so much of the world is doing. They see that Judaism teaches us how to make our lives as fulfilling as possible.

"That in turn serves as evidence that the Torah comes from a higher Source—from the Creator, who knows exactly what makes us tick."

At Hebrew University, Bracha walked into the dorms housing American students and knocked on random doors. "My first time at Hebrew U., my husband went with me," she recounts. "I was pregnant, and he was bearded and wearing his suit and black hat. People didn't know what to think. Moshe would immediately ask them if his wife could sit down. Of course, they'd welcome us in, and we'd start talking. After some conversation, many students expressed interest in experiencing a traditional Shabbos meal with a local family.

"Bais Yaakov girls from my neighborhood volunteered to line up families. We called it 'Friday Night Live,' which soon became famous. One week we had 70 students from Hebrew U. and 50 from Young Judea!

"College students love talking about relationships, so we also brought busloads from Hebrew U. to tour a mikveh and hear about the Torah's approach to intimacy."

The Zarets hosted all kinds of folks. "The university stipulated that sign-up lists be open to all, including non-Jews," Bracha explains. "But the families were expecting Jewish students. So my husband and I ended up with all the non-Jews. Once we hosted a Protestant minister, a priest, and a monk!"

Most of the Zarets' guests were Jewish students, however, and Bracha learned a lot from them. "I had failures and successes," she reports. "I used to be too intense, but I learned through my husband's example. He taught me to tone myself down and be more digestible. I also read tons of psychology books to understand people better."

Bracha was indefatigable. Her outreach work grew and grew, until she was employing 10 people (including a Spanish speaker to work with the many South American programs). She and her husband had become an institution, and it was time to give it a name. They decided on Mesoret Ameinu—"Tradition of Our People." Under their new banner, they and their staff introduced more and more students to Jewish observance. "To this day, I meet people who tell me their religious journey began when we met them on their campus or at the Kotel," Bracha says.

In 1986, after six years in Israel, Moshe was offered a place in the Lakewood Kollel of Los Angeles, and the *kollel* wanted Bracha to continue her efforts there as well. So the Zarets relocated.

Bracha began by contacting all the people from LA whom she'd met in Israel, bringing them to classes all over town, and inviting them for Shabbat. She initiated home study groups for non-religious women, as well as morning learning programs for marrieds (childcare provided) at the local Bais Yaakov, in Beverly Hills, and in the Valley. Moshe started a program for these women's husbands. Bracha then reached out to young, professional single women ("and any-where single women go, single men come," she said with a grin). She also organized one-on-one tutorials, and many tutors formed relationships with their students and invited them for Shabbat. She encouraged singles to study in Israel and connected couples to local rabbis and religious families. "Countless people became religious because of those pro-grams," Bracha relates. "Many of these men and women are now well-known in the Jewish community, with beautiful families of their own."

Meanwhile, Rabbi Dovid Refson, dean of Neve Yerusha-layim, spoke to famous philanthropist Zev Wolfson (of blessed memory) about Bracha. One day, after 10 years in Los Anglele, she heard that Zev's son, Aaron, was visiting and decided to pay him a surprise visit. "I dropped in af-ter Friday night dinner, bringing along my 20 non-religious Shabbat guests," she recounts. Aaron was impressed, and soon after she got a call from his father. Again, she was asked for a wish list. As fate would have it, she and her husband had just been invited to a Hillel Shabbat program at UCLA.

"UCLA was an amazing opportunity right in our back-yard—there were 3,000 Jewish students there," she notes. "So I told Mr. Wolfson I wanted to hire staff to work at UCLA. And he gave us the funding."

Bracha named her organization JAM—the Jew-ish Awareness Movement. "We brought tons of UCLA students to families for Shabbos," she recalls. "The hospitality was incredible—it was like a whole volunteer army! People loved opening their homes to non-*frum* people—they just hadn't known where to find them. And then I realized: This could be done in any *frum* community near a university. Mr. Wolfson was ready to put up the money. We just needed young couples on campus to bring in the students."

It wasn't easy finding couples to do this kind of *kiruv*. "*B'nei Torah* were cloistered—they didn't want to be involved with college students," Bracha says. "One young rabbi even hung up on me!

"I scoured the yeshivah world for talented *avrechim* and their wives. Besides being able to talk to secular college students, they had to be driven, focused, warm, articulate, and joyful—a tall order."

Bracha eventually found the people she was looking for, many of whom have since made a name for themselves in *kiruv* (including that rabbi who'd hung up on her!).

Within no time, JAM spread to universities throughout Southern California. Bracha herself traveled to these campuses, while her husband took over management and fundraising.

Thanks to Moshe, JAM built a multimillion-dollar outreach center on UCLA's Fraternity Row. Nightly classes and tutorials are held there, along with Shabbat meals and challah baking. On Shabbat, students meet religious people their own age and stay up till the wee hours talking and playing board games.

"The atmosphere is pleasant and relaxed," says Bracha. "Our center is a hub on campus, providing a home away from home for students and a peer community growing together."

Fifteen years after her initiation into *kiruv* at the Kotel, Bracha had inspired hundreds of individuals and couples to become religious. Never one to rest on her laurels, however, she decided to organize student vacations to vibrant Jewish communities.

Bracha started with a highly subsidized, 10-day visit to New York for about 40 students. Mornings were filled with classes by well-known outreach speakers, while afternoons were devoted to touring. Shabbat was spent with families in Monsey, north of the city. The trips proved so life-altering that the Zarets ran dozens of them.

One highlight of the program was attending a religious wedding. "We would contact a local religious caterer and ask who was getting married," Bracha recalls. "We'd then call the couple (generally *yeshivish* or *Chassidish*) and ask to bring some non-religious students to the *chuppah* and dancing. We were never refused. All these couples allowed 40 California college kids to crash their weddings! Though these students obviously came from a different world, everyone was so warm and welcoming. It was amazing."

Bracha recalls one particular wedding. "A female student was standing near the *mechitzah*, watching the men dance around the *chasan*, when she saw a familiar face—her religious cousin. It turned out she was related to the groom! Within minutes, his entire family surrounded her, warmly welcoming her into the family. As they talked more, they discovered that during World War II, the girl's grandfather had saved the *chasan*'s grandfather by helping him escape from prison. 'If not for your grandfather,' the *chasan's* father exclaimed, 'there would be no wedding!' It was incredible how that entire *Chassidish* clan embraced her. Even after she returned to LA, they kept inviting her to visit."

That young woman, Bracha says, became religious and lives in Israel with her husband and children. Her brother followed in her footsteps. "That happened many times," Bracha says. "A student would become *frum* through our organization, then one or more siblings followed, and sometimes the whole family."

The Zarets also started taking students to AIPAC (the American Israel Public Affairs Committee, a large pro-Israel lobby) in Washington, DC, combined with a Shabbat in Baltimore. They then launched a London trip. "Families put up students for an entire week," Bracha recounts. "In every city, the outpouring of help and positivity was phenomenal." They led trips to Poland as well, which provided a powerful dose of Jewish identity.

The overflowing hospitality offered by religious communities never ceased to move Bracha. "Once, in New York, there was a huge snowstorm, and our bus got stranded," she recalls. "Thirty students and I ventured out, trudging through the snow in search of alternative transportation. We finally found a pay phone (this was before cell phones), and I started making calls. People promptly came in their SUVs, braving the blizzard to take us all home to Brooklyn for the night. One family alone took 20 students! This kind of thing always brought me closer to Hashem and His Torah."

In 1996, the Zarets brought college kids to Israel for a full three weeks of learning, touring, and Shabbat in the Holy Land. The program quickly became central to the

JAM experience. "Participants were transformed," Bracha reports. "Much of that stemmed from the incredible hospitality we were shown. Everywhere we went, families took us in. People vied for the honor of hosting the whole group for a meal. Every event was held in a private home. I remember feeling, 'Mi k'amcha Yisrael' (Who is like Your people, Israel)!

"At the end of the trip, students always said they had never seen communities give so much. The kids were transfixed by the family life they saw—parents and children having fun together, relating to each other with love and respect. Even family dinners were a novelty to many. These encounters, along with the creation of a peer group and exposure to Torah wisdom, brought many hundreds of people back to Judaism."

Not everyone was ready for three weeks in Israel with daily Torah study, however. So starting in 2008, JAM partnered with Birthright, offering many young adults a 10-day tour with more Jewish content than they might otherwise have had.

Bracha owes her success not only to her inexhaustible energy, but to her perseverance, and the fact that she's never "off duty." "I once met a young woman on line at Ben Gurion airport for a flight to LA," she relates. "I engaged her in conversation and took her phone number. When we got back to California, I called and invited her for Shabbos. She couldn't come. So I called again. And again. And again. Finally she came. She was pursuing a Ph.D. in psychology and found the conversation very stimulating, so she came back. She's now religious, married with four children, and living in Jerusalem."

Decades later, outreach has become normative, and Bracha's is highly praised. "In the beginning, I was 'out of the box' and concerned about what people would think," she says. "But eventually I got tremendous support from the entire *frum* world, even *gedolim* such as Rav Avrohom Pam, Rav Yaakov Kamenetsky, and Rav Shmuel Kamenetsky. In Israel, a big *rav* named Asher Arieli knows my son-in-law and came to my grandson's *bris*. People were shocked that the rabbi came over to the women's side to say *mazal tov* and encourage me in my work." (She once sent a Hebrew-speaking student to the Arielis. "He was wearing a black leather jacket and riding a motorcycle. Today he has a beard and nine children.")

Bracha's operation was the first of its kind supported by the Wolfsons, but it has been far from the last. The family (along with philanthropist Eli Horn) made a massive investment in campus *kiruv* through Olami, a worldwide organization that has poured $100 million into outreach. It currently funds nearly 100 workers throughout North America. More and more young Jews are learning about their heritage—and it all started with one woman.

How did Bracha accomplish all of the above while raising a family? "I tended to go overboard," she admits. "The work was all-consuming, and at times I felt that my four children were getting the short end of the stick. But they seem to have survived, and even thrived, *baruch Hashem.*

"I also worried about their constant exposure to secular college students. But Rabbi Pam and Rabbi Shmuel Kamenetsky told me my kids would be protected in the merit of my important work. I can't explain why else they turned out so great (aside from my husband's wonderful influence). And our sons-in-law are gems, all wonderful *b'nei Torah.* My oldest daughter's husband is an extraordinary *talmid chacham*—a *rosh kollel* and *posek,* and a *talmid muvhak* of Rav Asher Weiss in Israel. All this from a Brooklyn cabbie's daughter!"

Always looking for more *kiruv* opportunities, Bracha has now come full circle and is once again involved in outreach in Israel. "We work with American college graduates who come on programs such as Masa ["Journey," an Israeli government initiative for young adults encouraging *aliyah*]. My daughter Chana is in charge. We also just hired a couple in Caesaria to run programs in Haifa, Netanya, and the Interdisciplinary Center in Herzliya. These places are *kiruv*'s new frontier."

Bracha's unflagging desire to share Judaism has always kept her moving, and thousands of people and their descendants who now lead rich Jewish lives are testimony to the power of this woman who has never slowed down. In changing the face of *kiruv*, Bracha Zaret has changed the Jewish people forever.

> People experience life as purposeful and worthwhile if they have an elevated spirit faithful to the image of God—the image in which they were uniquely created—and to their inner individuality. (Rabbi Abraham Isaac Kook)

Chapter Ten

Sunny Disposition, Black Belt

SUNNY REMEMBERS THE day clearly. Age 9½, she was in her back yard with her younger siblings. Suddenly an 11-year-old boy two heads taller than she appeared in the yard next door.

"Dirty Jews," he sneered.

"Oh, yeah?" Sunny countered. "Wanna fight about it?"

"Yeah, and I'm gonna beat you up!"

Before the young anti-Semite knew it, a reverse crescent kick to the face knocked him to the ground. Shocked at her own power, Sunny ran into her house and promptly threw up.

Fortunately, Sunny rarely had to use her martial arts skills on the street. But she's still using them on behalf of the Jewish community.

Born in 1977, Sunny Levi grew up in Chicago's Peterson Park neighborhood. Her family was on the less observant end of the Modern Orthodox spectrum. She was the third of six children, and a tomboy.

One fateful day, her life took an unexpected turn. Her mother had enrolled her 5-year-old brother in a Taekwondo class. But the little boy disliked the discipline, was scared of the teacher, and ran out of the first lesson sobbing. The program wouldn't refund his tuition but offered to apply it to another child in the family. So Sunny stepped up to the plate. It was love at first kick. She was 8 years old.

"Looking back, I'm not sure what drew me to this ancient Korean martial art," she wrote in a 2009 article for *Chabad. org*. "Maybe it was my teachers' insistence that nothing is impossible as long as we don't give up. Maybe it was the confidence and sense of achievement I felt after training so hard. Or maybe Taekwondo was an outlet for the stresses of growing up with a severely disabled older brother.

"All I knew is that I was intrigued by the intensity. I even enjoyed the push-ups, torturous stretches, and strict, army-like rules." Something in the rigor of Taekwondo spoke to Sunny's soul.

As she grew, Sunny had two dreams. The first was to compete in the Olympics. To that end, she took four to five Taekwondo classes a week. By age 13, she had a black belt and was competing nationally. By 14, in addition to her grueling training schedule, she was teaching Taekwondo. Sunny eventually made it to the Junior Olympics and the Pam Am Cup. By the time she enrolled in DePaul University in Chicago, she was being coached by a former world champion.

As a martial artist, Sunny was a force to be reckoned with. She recalls one story from when she was 16:

"My Taekwondo class was taught by a master 6th-degree black belt who'd come to the U.S. from Korea to train us. One day, we each had to fight him. I was the only girl and just 5'3", so he didn't consider me much of a challenge. But I surprised him with a kick in the jaw—hard. He paled and looked furious. I was so scared—I thought he was going to kill me! Instead, he told me I was the only American ever to kick him in the face. He was impressed, and I won his respect. He couldn't chew for a week, but we've been friends ever since.

"Only two other times have I injured someone. One was in summer camp, when a boy picked a fight with me just to prove that a female black belt meant nothing. I won—and I think I also broke his knee, because the next time I saw him, he was on crutches and wouldn't speak to me. The other time, a guy was hitting on me and wouldn't leave me alone, so I put him in his place. Otherwise, I'm a peaceful person."

Sunny's second dream was to become an actress. She had an agent and even appeared in commercials as well as independent and industrial films.

In short, life was full of promise.

Then Sunny's father was diagnosed with cancer. Suddenly her goals seemed insignificant. She started thinking about God and the meaning of life, questioning everything from the bottom up. Eventually Sunny realized that her career aspirations conflicted with many of her values. She witnessed how low her fellow actresses stooped to be "discovered" and land a coveted part. She experienced her agent's rage when she turned down a McDonald's commercial requiring her to eat unkosher food, and when she passed up a role in a movie filming over Sukkot. And she felt sick every time her Taekwondo coach yelled at her to kick faster, as if that were the greatest thing she could do in life.

Around this time Sunny met her husband, Daniel, a Jew who was into Buddhism and studying comparative religion at Harvard. The connection was immediate, but because they lived over 800 miles apart, they remained pen-pals for four years. Once they finally started dating, they were engaged in no time.

Sunny and Daniel began their life together in Chicago and soon welcomed their first child. However, having married with the understanding that Daniel would give Judaism a chance, they picked up and went to Israel for a year so he could study Torah. That year turned into four, during which Sunny also attended as many Torah classes as she could. They returned to Chicago with three small children and committed to living full Torah lives.

Master Sunny Levi is now a 6th-degree black belt (having more than lived her motto: "A black belt is a white belt that never gave up") and has integrated her passion for martial arts with a Torah way of life. At Sunny's Martial Arts and Fitness, she teaches Jewish children as well as women and teenage girls. Sunny is also a certified personal trainer, teaching women's yoga, strength training, cardio kickboxing, and self-defense. But her main focus is on kids.

"My goal is to brings youngsters closer to Hashem by building self-discipline, self-empowerment, self-awareness, self-esteem, and self-respect," she writes. "Through martial arts, I help kids know themselves, what they're made of, and what they stand for. By training hard and striving to progress, they can achieve a level of perseverance and patience that strengthens not only their bodies but their minds and hearts."

The three oldest of Sunny's six children—Eden Yisraella (born in 2004), Moshe Ohr (born in 2005), and Gedaliah Avichai (born in 2007)— have black belts and help her teach. She also coaches her students and kids in small, local tournaments (the large ones are on Shabbat, and in any case, she discourages the high level competing she experienced). She participates in women's demo teams with the approval of her rabbi, who told her that doing so is a *kiddush Hashem*. And she's working toward the coveted 10th-degree black belt.

Then there's Camp Kale. Every summer, Sunny runs a mini-camp out of her house, focusing on health, fitness, and creativity. "We make wholesome foods and learn about their benefits—no junk food is allowed," she says. "We do a variety of exercises, including yoga, kickboxing, toning, weight lifting, and, of course, Taekwondo. We do art, skits, and improvisation. And we practice gratitude, so our minds and souls will be as healthy as our bodies."

Sunny attributes her ability to be "out of the box" to her parents. "They were hippies who became *ba'alei teshuvah* but remained free spirits," she recalls. "They did their own thing. So being different was our norm, and I was used to marching to the beat of my own drum."

Yet the road to becoming a martial artist wasn't always smooth. "It's not ladylike to do martial arts," she was told, or "You must be very violent if you like that stuff." Later the refrain became "Who would want to marry you??" While these comments could sting, Sunny knew she was doing what was best for her. Moreover, she believed that her soul mate wouldn't be scared off by her black belt.

Now that she's married and established in the community, Sunny's rarely criticized—at least not to her face. Instead, she hears jokes like "I bet your husband never steps out of line!" (Actually, he's her biggest fan.)

"People don't understand the depth of martial arts," Sunny explains. "A martial artist doesn't misuse the art. Yes, I can fight and defend myself, but the more 'dangerous' I become, the more self-control and patience I need. Real martial arts isn't just about muscles, speed, and stamina. It's about inner strength."

Sunny sees Taekwondo as spiritually relevant to many aspects of life. "We all get knocked down," she points out. "We have to learn how to fall without getting hurt and how to get up quickly. Doing the Taekwondo motions can help us with those inevitable emotional dives."

Likewise, "Sparring requires not only skill but much thought. The same is true for any fight we encounter in our lives. We need speed, timing, and power but also good strategy."

And as for smashing through wood or cement with one's bare hands or feet, for which martial artists are perhaps most famous: "Board breaking is a great metaphor for conquering things in life, getting past difficult situations, and overcoming challenges. Taekwondo teaches that if we can visualize it, we can do it. Then we focus our energy and break through."

How does Sunny negotiate being different from most other women in her community? She admits it's a little tricky, and not only because of her martial arts. With her dress (colorful and sporty), the food she eats ("completely natural and green"), her home births, and her general way of being, she doesn't quite fit in. But what's most important to her is being with people who are serious about serving Hashem. "I may be 'out of the box' in many aspects of my lifestyle," she says, "but my community and I are in the same 'spiritual box,' and that's what counts.

"Being different can be isolating and even embarrassing, but most of the time I feel free and happy, because I know I'm living my truth and doing what Hashem created me to do. When I remember that I'm a unique person with unique skills, I understand that I'm not meant to be like everyone else. We all have different missions, and I'm glad mine is to be a *frum*, female martial arts instructor. I can't imagine doing anything else."

One of the greatest benefits of Sunny's "marching to the beat of her own drum" has been the impact on her relationship with Hashem and Torah. "I use my strengths to connect to Hashem in creative ways, such as through movement. Being so in my body makes it easier for me to find God in the physical world. At the same time, my training has taught me how to quiet the mind, which has greatly benefited my prayer."

Sunny concludes: "I've found a path that works for me, that's right for my soul and personality. It helps keep my spirituality alive."

POSTSCRIPT:

In addition to teaching and training in Taekwondo, Sunny now works as a martial arts therapist with Kids Kicking Cancer (see chapter 7, "Power, Peace, Purpose"). Once a week, she teaches hospitalized children how to use breathing and meditation techniques to alleviate pain and anxiety. With at least one patient, she has also put her acting talents to good use.

"When this little girl saw my karate outfit, she didn't want to work with me," Sunny recounts. 'I don't like ninjas,' she announced. 'Okay,' I said, 'what *do* you like?' 'Ballerinas,' she replied. So I told her I was actually a ballerina wearing a ninja costume. I did a few funny dance moves and acted really girly to win her over. It worked.

"The following week, when she met me in the hall, she was so excited that she ran toward me, almost knocking down her IV pole. She told me she'd had some difficult treatments, but she'd used the breathing I'd taught her, and it really helped.

"She still doesn't like my outfit, but every time I visit her, I go back into that girly role, and she happily does 'ballerina breathing' with me."

Both physically and spiritually, with all my abilities, talents, and potential, I am unique in the universe. Of all those alive today, there's no other me.

Throughout history, there never was another me, and there never will be.

So the Master of the Universe must have sent me here on a special mission that I alone—in all my uniqueness—can accomplish. (Rabbi Shlomo Wolbe)

Chapter Eleven

Funny, You Don't Look Zooish

I MAGINE A CHASSIDIC boy, wearing sidelocks and traditional Chassidic garb—but with a 12-foot-long python around his neck.

If you can't picture that, you haven't visited the Biblical Museum of Natural History in Beit Shemesh, founded and directed by animal-lover Rabbi Dr. Natan Slifkin.*

Rabbi Slifkin was born in 1975, the youngest of five, and raised in the Orthodox community of Manchester. With a physicist father, he received a strong education in both Torah and secular subjects. But what interested him most wasn't taught in school, nor is it common in religious circles.

---

* Many years ago, Rabbi Slifkin was involved in a much-publicized controversy over Torah and science, but his zoological educational programs are approved by communities across the Orthodox spectrum.

"Ever since I was a child, I was obsessed with animals," Rabbi Slifkin recounts. "The animal kingdom is so diverse, with creatures of every shape, size, color, texture, ability, and behavior—it was mesmerizing!" As he grew, so did his pet collection, ranging from hamsters to parrots to lizards. His father encouraged his passion, while his mother tolerated it. "She allowed me whatever pets I wanted, as long as they were caged," he relates. "The only ones she vetoed were snakes and tarantulas—so I hid them in my closet." His bar mitzvah teacher, whom he remembers fondly, told him that when he grew up, he should write a book about animals in the Torah.

Unfortunately, Manchester offered no formal opportunities for Natan to develop his interest. Beyond his home menagerie, he contented himself with books and documentaries about animals—and dreaming of his own zoo.

In Natan's late teens, with adulthood looming, his desire to work with animals drew criticism. "Be realistic," he was advised. "Choose a practical career, like computer programming."

At age 18, Natan and his family made *aliyah*, and he entered yeshivah. Putting his preoccupation with animals behind him, he dedicated himself to Torah study and a future in Jewish education.

Then one day, when he was 21, Natan had an inspiration: *Why not look into what the Torah says about animals?* He discovered an incredible wealth of material dealing with all aspects of zoology: identifying the animals in the Bible, understanding their symbolism, clarifying the laws that apply to them, and more. "It was absolutely fascinating! I couldn't get enough. And the more I learned, the more I wanted to share my knowledge with others."

Initially, no one took him seriously. His parents had always encouraged his individuality, but neither they nor his his rabbis understood the value of studying Biblical zoology. Then he joined a volunteer training course at the Jerusalem Biblical Zoo and began promoting the zoo's biblical aspect. His programs were an instant hit, and he promptly took them on the road, receiving equally enthusiastic responses at zoos all over the U.S.

Concurrently, Natan studied in various yeshivot, culminating in the famous Mir Yeshivah. He then joined the faculty at Ohr Somayach, where he received rabbinic ordination. Eventually the time came to find a mate.

"When I was 24, someone told me I'd never get married, because *frum* girls dislike animals," Rabbi Slifkin relates. "So when I started dating, I hid my passion. But ultimately I realized that love of animals was a major part of me and it was foolish to pretend otherwise. While I honestly believed I had outgrown pets, I decided to feature a photo of me on my website shaking 'hands'/flippers with a sea lion. If that put a girl off, I figured, there was no point in meeting her."

Fortunately, a young woman from Los Angeles named Tali wasn't put off. He and Tali married and settled in Ramat Beit Shemesh.

Rabbi Slifkin continued his biblical zoology programs, but he wasn't satisfied. "Zoos are great, but they don't make for a very focused educational environment," he says. "They're outdoors, which means lots of distractions and weather challenges. In addition, even the Jerusalem Biblical

Zoo lacks the right exhibits for a biblical zoology experience. Also, zoos offer few opportunities to touch or handle animals. I knew I needed something different."

During this time, Rabbi Slifkin's reputation spread. He appeared in Animal Planet's 2010 documentary *Beasts of the Bible* and spoke at conferences about Torah and science. His next step was clear. "Everyone at those conferences had a doctorate but me," he notes, "so I felt inadequate. I also realized that, if I ever opened the kind of institution I envisioned, a doctorate would be greatly advantageous. And I wondered how academic studies would complement my yeshivah background." With his extensive religious education and publications, Rabbi Slifkin was fast-tracked into a master's program at the Lander Institute in Jerusalem, where he earned an M.A. in Jewish thought and law. He then began working on his Ph.D. in Jewish history at Bar-Ilan University.

For years, Rabbi Slifkin had been collecting specimens for a projected biblical animal museum, but getting it off the ground took enormous work. The biggest challenge was finding donors who identified with his mission. Thankfully, the funding came through.

By the time the museum was ready to open, Rabbi Slifkin had amassed an impressive amount of material, with sources ranging from Alaska to Australia. "Some of our most extraordinary exhibits, such as the skeleton of an extinct giant cave bear, were donated by private collectors. Much of the taxidermy originated in Israeli zoos. As for the live animals, some were confiscated by the Israel Nature and

Parks Authority from people keeping them illegally, while most were obtained from a variety of zoos and exotic wildlife dealers."

Some creatures previously inhabited the Slifkin home. After their wedding, the Slifkins had visited a pet shop, where a baby rabbit melted Tali's heart. "It was all downhill from there!" Rabbi Slifkin says with a grin. He and his family acquired quite a few "housemates"—and not all stayed in their cages. "My wife was once woken at night by a video switched on by an escaped chinchilla," Rabbi Slifkin relates. "Then there was the morning my daughter went into the bathroom and was greeted by a frantically flapping fruit bat!" Eventually, all these "boarders" were moved to the museum—"much to my wife's relief," he notes. (While Tali doesn't share her husband's love of animals, she enjoys them from a distance and greatly appreciates his work. I personally commend her for being such a good sport.)

Rabbi Slifkin had also been accumulating taxidermy specimens in his house. "My youngest daughter was never scared at night," he reports, "because she felt protected by the stuffed wolf, cheetah, and hyena in her bedroom!" These, too, were relocated to the museum.

The Biblical Museum of Natural History opened in 2014. It's a fascinating place, displaying a wealth of mammals, birds, reptiles, amphibians, and insects mentioned in the Bible. Large animals are dead and stuffed, while smaller ones are quite alive and can often be handled.

But this part-zoo is first and foremost a Torah education center, demonstrating that, in Rabbi Slifkin's words, "Judaism relates to all aspects of life, including nature." Visitors experience first-hand the living creatures mentioned in the Bible and Talmud, which were an integral part of life in ancient Israel, figure prominently in Jewish law, and convey Jewish values. By inspiring awe and appreciation for the animals of the Land of Israel, the Biblical Museum of Natural History makes the Bible and Judaism come alive.

Exhibits include *Introduction to Biblical Natural History*, *Biblical Scenes*, *Beasts of Prey*, *Kosher Creatures*, *Eight Sh'ratzim* (small, creeping animals), and *Wonders of Creation*, this last encompassing such extraordinary creatures as the basilisk (a lizard that runs on water), the mudskipper (an amphibious fish), and the duck-billed platypus. In addition, the museum houses the world's largest assortment of horns and shofars, plus a five-foot-long narwhal tooth (once thought to be a unicorn horn). Finally, there's a petting zoo, featuring small, furry animals, 10 types of kosher birds, and a giant tortoise.

"Since the museum is full of animals, adults initially think it's just for kids, rather than a serious study center," Rabbi Slifkin says. "Of course, once people tour the place, they understand."

One remarkable aspect of the Biblical Museum of Natural History is the diversity of its visitors. "We get everything from Chassidic to Amish," the rabbi reports. "I think we have the broadest reach of any educational institution in Israel. Our program is suitable for everyone. We even get very religious groups that won't go to Israeli zoos because they're secular institutions open on Shabbat."

The museum tour provides an especially valuable learning experience for children who have no contact with animals and no idea how to interact with them. "Some kids don't realize animals are living creatures with feelings," Rabbi Slifkin observes. "When a child bangs on a cage to make an animal move, I ask how he would like it if someone banged on *his* house. Kids are taken aback by this question, but they grasp the concept. When they want to know if the turtle, lizard, or snake bites, I tell them that if they treat the animal with respect, it will reciprocate. They understand and handle it with care."

Through his museum, Rabbi Slifkin has "infected" countless others with his fascination with animals. "People gasp in wonder at the various exhibits, deepening their appreciation of both Torah and nature," he says proudly. "Secular Jews learn about an unexpected aspect of their Jewish identity, and religious Jews enrich their connection to Torah."

Rabbi Slifkin has rounded up a talented and devoted staff. All are Torah-observant, and some even speak Yiddish. Aside from dealing with the occasional escaped animal, they've faced emergencies such as rushing a hyrax to a veterinary hospital for a C-section on *erev Pesach*!

Does Rabbi Slifkin miss the numerous animals that used to occupy his home? "Actually, it's something of a relief not having to care for them anymore," he admits, "since the museum staff does that." But the rabbi hasn't totally kicked the habit: "Of course, we still have a few outside—just some turtles, hyraxes, ducks, and pheasants."

Thanks to a successful fundraising campaign, a much larger facility is being built to house the museum. Its inauguration is planned for early 2020.

Meanwhile, in 2016, Rabbi Slifkin received his Ph.D. His dissertation was entitled *Rabbinic Encounters with Zoology in the 19th Century*. Not long afterward, he published his magnum opus, *The Torah Encyclopedia of the Animal Kingdom*—which, upon returning to Manchester after a 24-year absence, he presented to his former bar mitzvah teacher in an emotional reunion.

In addition to his museum work, Rabbi Slifkin leads African safaris showcasing biblical wildlife no longer found in the Land of Israel. "We go to South Africa, Botswana, and Zimbabwe," he informs me. "It's the trip of a lifetime. There's nothing like sailing down the Chobe river alongside hippos, crocodiles, and elephants."

For some people, however, the ultimate encounter with the animals of the Bible is getting to eat them. Rabbi Slifkin has hosted several Biblical feasts—all fundraisers— serving such delicacies as dove and pigeon consommé, venison liver *pâté*, smoked kingklip, guineafowl, whole roasted quails, slow-cooked cow udders (minus the milk), Asian water buffalo, turkey animelles (don't ask), and the kicker: kosher locusts*—either chocolate-covered or carmelized. (Diners should remove the legs and wings first, and be warned that, according to one brave banquet participant, they may be "gritty" and leave "various elements of exoskeleton clinging to the tongue and teeth." Yum.)

With all due respect to exotic tours and cuisine, the Biblical Museum of Natural History remains Rabbi Slifkin's crowning achievement. By following his "animal instincts," he has created a one-of-a-kind opportunity to appreciate a beautiful part of God's world in a Torah context. As he explains, "My parents conveyed a strong message of doing what you believe in, even if it makes you different from everyone else." Looking back on those years when he thought he no longer needed animals, he comments: "I'm very pleased that I came to my senses!"

> The generation of the Tower of Babel lived in harmony only because society was monolithic. God therefore created different languages, so humanity could acknowledge and appreciate difference. True peace is achieved when, living in a world of diversity, we learn from one another and respect individuality. (Rabbi Yochanan Zweig)

---

* Most Jewish communities have lost the Sinaitic tradition regarding which locusts are kosher. May these Jews adopt the tradition of those who retained it? Halachic authorities disagree.

Chapter Twelve
A Light unto the Nations

ANY POWER THAT will exist in the complete redemption will enter the world little by little in the preceding period, which we are now in. One of those redemptive powers is that of reaching out to the nations of the world. — Rabbi Hillel Rivlin of Shklov (disciple of the Vilna Gaon), *Kol Ha Tor*

Rivkah Lambert Adler was born in 1959 and raised in a middle-class town on Long Island, outside of New York City. Her mother and father were first-generation Americans whose parents had emigrated from Eastern Europe as youngsters. By the time Rivkah, the second of three children, was growing up, her family had little more than a basic Jewish identity. "All the Jewish kids in my neighborhood went to public school," she relates. "While the boys also went to afternoon Hebrew school, most of the girls, including me, got no religious education at all. I knew I was Jewish, but it was irrelevant."

Rivkah always felt a bit different from her peers. "Even as a child, I was an independent thinker," she recalls. "Racial epithets were pretty common and socially acceptable then, but I objected to them. When I was older, a lot of kids were smoking marijuana, but I never did. In general, I felt no need to act like everyone else.

"I also had deeper interests. I don't remember a time when I wasn't attracted to what my daughters call DMCs—deep, meaningful conversations. When my parents invited friends over to socialize, the women talked about children and clothes, and the men, about sports and cars, but I found both conversations equally boring. I was energized by talking about life stories, feelings, and most of all, ideas."

Academically oriented, Rivkah loved school. "I used to play school with friends," she remembers, "and I was always the teacher." After graduating high school with honors, she earned a B.A. in speech communication from the University of Maryland, then pursued a master's in education. Her first job, her graduate assistantship, was as an academic advisor. "The students were all older than I was," she recounts, "but I really enjoyed answering their questions and guiding them, and I loved the academic environment. I also quickly learned that if you know what you're talking about, people take you seriously."

After receiving her master's, Rivkah began working in university administration and embarked upon part-time study for her Ph.D. Seeking a roommate, she searched the classified ads in the *Baltimore Jewish Times*—and while skimming other sections of the paper, she read of Jewish holidays she knew nothing about. Her curiosity piqued, she soon discovered a new interest: Judaism.

Rivkah signed up for an Introduction to Judaism class sponsored by the Baltimore Board of Rabbis. "The course was intended for prospective converts," she notes. "That's how little I knew." Most of the teachers were Conservative and Reform rabbis. Rivkah learned about the Bible, Jewish holidays, the Jewish lifecycle, and more. Upon completing the program, she celebrated her bat mitzvah in a Reform congregation.

Feeling more Jewish than ever, Rivkah attended a Jewish event featuring a "Test Your Jewish IQ" booth. But "I didn't get a single question right," she recollects. "The rabbi running the booth [an Orthodox *kiruv* activist] offered to set me up with a study partner. I agreed—largely because I assumed that only men knew anything about Judaism, and I was hoping to meet someone."

Her partner, however, turned out to be a pregnant young woman named Dena. "I thought she was undergoing chemotherapy, because she was wearing a wig," Rivkah remembers.

"I spent my first real Shabbat with Dena and her family. She helped me learn *alef-bet*, taught me how to celebrate the Jewish holidays, gave me my first *shalach manos*, and so much more."

At the same time, the first of what Rivkah calls her "three great passions in Jewish life" came to the fore: the role of women in Judaism. "From the moment I began learning about Orthodoxy, I felt conflicted about women's limited participation in certain aspects of it," she recalls. "I spent years struggling, reading everything about women in

Judaism that I could get my hands on. Eventually, I discovered *The Moon's Lost Light* by Devorah (Heshelis) Fastag, which shifted my paradigm. This book gave me a nuanced understanding of how the current situation developed and how it will eventually change."

Despite her issues, Rivkah continued learning about Judaism. In 1988, she married. "I wasn't yet committed to keeping anything," she says. "Dena encouraged me to go to the *mikveh* before my wedding, so I went on a lark, just to have the experience.

"I never intended to become observant. It was just a process of learning and trying out different Jewish experiences. But when I finally understood that God wrote the Torah as a guidebook for Jewis to live by, I could no longer pick and choose."

Rivkah completed her Ph.D. in 1993. In 1996, newly divorced and with two children, she married Rabbi Elan Adler. Several years later, fusing her love of learning and teaching with her love of Judaism, Rivkah became the director of adult education at Baltimore's Center for Jewish Education. Observant, married to a rabbi, and occupying an important position in the Jewish community, she had seemingly "arrived" religiously.

A few years earlier, however, Rivkah's second great Jewish passion had arisen: Israel, and specifically *aliyah*. "On September 11, 2001, it became clear to me that America was merely a host country and it was time to go home," she says. "I spent untold hours learning everything I could about living in Israel. I even ran a successful *chug* helping Baltimore families make the move." Although Rivkah was ready to pick up and go, Elan wasn't prepared to leave his pulpit. After nine long years, "Hashem finally said it was our turn," as Rivkah puts it, and in July 2010, she and her family made *aliyah*. They settled in the Jerusalem suburb of Ma'ale Adumim. Rivkah had come home not only spiritually but physically.

But her real life's work was yet to begin.

In Israel, Rivkah's third Jewish passion took center stage.

"I had long been fascinated by the whole concept of *geulah*, the world's redemption," she recounts. "I wanted to make *aliyah* because I understood the return of the Jewish people to the Land of Israel as part of the *geulah* process. And I had come to realize that women's changing roles are also connected to the redemption. Back in the U.S., I had even started a Yahoo group (now a Facebook group) called 'Geula Watch,' a place to share *divrei Torah*, links to *shiurim*, and more about this fascinating topic.

"One important work dealing with the *geulah* is *Kol HaTor* (The Voice of the Turtledove), written in the early 1800s. Devorah Fastag was very influenced by it. Now that I was in Israel, I had the privilege of meeting her, and she learned it with me—twice. It sung to my soul. I felt as if I was accessing a higher level of existence. I discovered that the world is so much more complex than we're aware of, with so much more happening spiritually than we realize."

Gradually, Rivkah's passion for the *geulah* became known. In 2015, she was invited to write news stories for predominantly Christian audiences about the fulfillment of biblical prophecies related to the *geulah*. Her articles on the ingathering of the exiles, the strengthening of women's leadership, and more appeared in *Breaking Israel News*, the *Jerusalem Post*, the *Jewish Press*, and *Jewish Values Online*.

Through her writing, Rivkah came into contact with a whole new population: people from Christian backgrounds who were connected to Torah. "It was eye-opening," she says. "These people study the weekly Torah portion, welcome Shabbat on Friday at sunset, observe the Jewish holidays, and avoid pork and shellfish. They're integrating a new respect for Torah into their religious lives, even as they retain some kind of belief in Christianity. Often, they trace their interest in Judaism to their understanding that Jesus was a Jew and had himself lived by the Torah. Unlike missionaries, they look up to Jews as fulfilling an essential purpose in the world, and they want to learn from us.

"I was also reading a lot," Rivkah recalls, "and texts about the Torah's view of gentiles kept jumping out at me. I was being drawn into a fascinating new realm, that of the Jewish people's relationship with the non-Jewish world."

Encountering more and more gentiles who sincerely wanted to study Jewish wisdom, Rivkah embarked upon a daring new career: teaching non-Jews about Judaism. "Given that my professional background is in educational administration, and that I'm a rabbi's wife and have been teaching Torah (on my humble level) for 20 years, responding to the desire for Torah teachings on the part of non-Jews felt like a natural next step," she says. "It's not something I chose. It chose me. Without question, Hashem put me in this job."

Teaching Torah to gentiles is often considered controversial.* The Talmud (*Sanhedrin* 59a) states that non-Jews are forbidden to learn Torah, and therefore Jews must not cause them to sin by teaching them. Yet Rivkah cites a responsum by Rabbi Yechiel Michel Charlop (1889-1974), founding president of the Rabbinical Council, later renamed the Rabbinical Council of America (RCA). Rabbi Charlop maintains that most rabbis have historically applied both these prohibitions only to the Oral Torah, not the Written. Today, however, the Oral Torah is widely available in print (even in English), so non-Jews can learn it on their own. Consequently, he rules, teaching them is no longer prohibited.**

Other contemporary rabbis go even farther, opining that teaching Torah to gentiles may now be not only permitted but even desirable. One such rabbinic authority, whom Rivkah follows regarding this issue, is Rabbi Yitzchak Ginsburgh, an American-born Israeli scholar affiliated with the Chabad movement.

Rabbi Ginsburgh writes that there have been three revolutions in Torah learning. Each began with abrogating a prohibition out of necessity, and each led to a dramatic increase in Torah scholarship.

The first revolution was the transcription of the Oral Torah, around the year 200, lest these teachings be lost amid Jewish national exile and persecution. Yet the recording of the Mishnah, the compilation of Judaism's oral tradition, resulted in the development of the enormous, rich, and

---

* Any Jew wishing to teach non-Jews about Judaism should consult a rabbi for guidelines.

** See Rabbi Charlop's *Chof Yamim, Chagigah* 1:70.

ever-expanding corpus of Jewish literature that dominates Torah study today.

The second revolution was the public funding of Torah education. Intended to preserve Jewish literacy, this move ended up creating a whole segment of society devoted to full-time Torah study and instruction, ensuring that both would not only survive but flourish.

The third revolution was the establishment of formal Jewish education for women with the launch of the Bais Yaakov movement in the early 20th century. While initially meant simply to keep girls religious, this effort has resulted in many highly educated women making uniquely valuable contributions to Torah study.

Rabbi Ginsburgh believes we're now are on the brink of a fourth revolution: teaching Torah to non-Jews. He sees gentiles' growing interest in Torah as a clear sign of redemption, necessitating our introducing them to the full range of Torah teachings. Rabbi Ginsburgh writes:[*]

> We are all familiar with the words of the prophet Isaiah: "And many nations will go, and they will say, 'Let us ascend the mountain of God to the Temple of the God of Jacob, and He will teach us of His ways, and we will follow His path,' for from Zion shall the Torah emerge [to non-Jews], and the word of God from Jerusalem" (Isaiah 2:3). Jeremiah also prophesied, "To you will come nations from the extremes of the earth, and they will say, 'Only falsity did our forefathers teach us'" (Jeremiah 16:19). The prophet

---

[*] www.inner.org/chassidut/the-fourth-revolution-in-torah-learning.

Zephaniah heralded an era when, "...I will convert the peoples to a pure language, so that all of them call the name of God, to worship Him with one accord" (Zephaniah 3:9).

A non-Jew is commanded to study and observe the seven Noahide commandments. As the Talmud states explicitly, "Even a non-Jew who engages in Torah [studying things that pertain to the seven mitzvot] is like a high priest" (*Baba Kama* 38a). It is the task of the Jewish people to teach and disseminate the Torah of the Noahides to all [...], as Maimonides and others explain (see *Hilchot Melachim* 8:10; *Tosfot Yom-Tov, Avot* 3:14). The Lubavitcher Rebbe stressed that in our generation, the world is ready, and it is time for us to put this into practice. [...]

But keeping the seven Noahide mitzvot does not suffice. This level of Torah study alone cannot fully realize the idea of *tikkun olam*. [...] The nations of the world can only recognize the Torah as the source of all the sparks of truth that their religions contain if they are exposed to the entire Torah in all its glory. They must study Torah in a way that reveals its depth and its profound relevance to their own lives.

Rivkah is realizing this vision. "Non-Jews have unprecedented access to Torah in print and online," she points out. "What they lack are teachers to guide them. If they're interested enough to study on their own, we must teach them." To that end, she has helped create classes and one-day seminars. She makes short videos and teaches online. And she writes news stories about the increasing number of people worldwide coming closer to Torah, Israel, and the Jewish nation.

"Gentile interest in authentic Torah is growing exponentially," she says. "Non-Jews eager to learn contact me every day, and I try to answer their questions.

"There's no formal training in this kind of bridge-building. I'm learning as I go. As a major networker, I meet people on this path and listen to their stories. I collaborate with those who've been doing this work longer than I. And I use my skills—writing, teaching, organizing events—to amplify the message that the time has come for Jews to start teaching Torah to non-Jews."

In 2017, Rivkah published *Ten From The Nations: Torah Awakening Among Non-Jews*, including first-person accounts by 37 non-Jews moving toward Torah and 12 Jews reaching out to them. "I chose this title," she says, "because I believe we're beginning to see the fulfillment of a prophecy from Zechariah:[*] 'So said the Lord of Hosts: In those days, it will come to pass that ten men out of all the languages of the nations will take hold of the skirt of a Jewish man, saying, 'Let us go with you, for we have heard God is with you.'

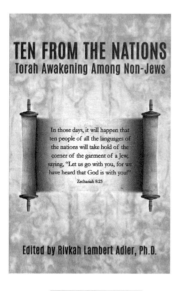

TEN FROM THE NATIONS
Torah Awakening Among Non-Jews

In those days, it will happen that ten people of all the languages of the nations will take hold of the corner of the garment of a Jew, saying, "Let us go with you, for we have heard that God is with you!"
Zechariah 8:23

Edited by Rivkah Lambert Adler, Ph.D.

---

* 8:23.

"I used to think that being a light to the nations* meant simply that Jews were to create a perfect society in the Land of Israel, which the rest of the world would admire and emulate. But the idea is much deeper. We have to teach the world that the universe has only one God and that His directions for humanity are expressed in the Torah. We must also help solve humanity's problems, both physical and spiritual. To achieve these goals, we can't just be who we are, we have to interact with non-Jews."

Rivkah has no interest in converting anyone to Judaism. "Most of the people I work with don't want to become Jews, and there's no reason they should," she emphasizes. "I'm just trying to respond to the need described by the prophet Amos:** 'Behold, days are coming, says the Lord God, and I will send famine into the land, not a famine for bread nor a thirst for water, but to hear the word of the Lord.' I'm simply bringing Torah teachings, as authentically as I can, to non-Jews who hunger and thirst for them."

Rabbi Ginsburgh believes that teaching gentiles will contribute to *Jewish* spiritual growth as well. He writes:

> Teaching Torah to non-Jews is a great challenge to any individual who takes it upon himself [or herself]. But encountering people who are far removed from Torah will bring him [or her] into contact with questions and new perspectives that will rejuvenate his [or her] relationship with the Torah and infuse it with new motivation. We can already see this happen with

---

* Isaiah 49:6.

** 8:11.

people involved in Jewish outreach, in Chabad houses and the like.

But teaching the Torah to non-Jews offers far greater value to the Jewish people. It is no secret that modern Judaism is suffering from a deep crisis. Many individuals (and even groups) have distanced themselves from Torah study and even from their Jewish identity. One outstanding reason for this crisis is [that] they identify with universalism. In contrast, Judaism [seemingly] functions as a national religion that [...] has nothing to offer the rest of humanity. Perceiving Judaism through the prism of teaching the Torah to non-Jews will open the minds and hearts of many distant Jews to see the Torah in a new light.

Rivkah has indeed gained much from teaching gentiles. "Non-Jews are very Bible-based," she explains. "I take my own *Tanach* study more seriously because of their questions. More importantly, I now see so many biblical references to the nations that I once overlooked, so I see Judaism's universal messages much more clearly. I used to think of Torah as belonging exclusively to the Jewish people. Now I view things differently."

What has given Rivkah the strength to follow such a different path, one that other Orthodox Jews may frown upon?

"Long before I started teaching Torah to non-Jews, I had my own ideas about how things should be done in the Jewish world," Rivkah says, "so I acquired a reputation for being outspoken.

"For example, I wasn't happy about the lack of opportunity for women to celebrate Simchat Torah. So a few years ago, I started 'The Parsha Slam.' About 45 women actively participate. We divide up all the *parashiyot*, and each woman prepares a one-minute talk about her *parashah* (or, in a few cases, her two *parashiyot*), so that in about an hour and a quarter, we review all of *Chumash*. At first this activity was held in a private home, but now, since another 55 or so women come just to listen, we meet in a synagogue social hall. It feels like a more meaningful alternative to what's currently available for women.

"As you see, if a practice doesn't work for me, I simply try something different. That same can-do attitude has enabled me to do something as different as teaching Torah to non-Jews."

Rivkah attributes much of her belief in herself to the fact that she has never been "standard." "Nothing about my background is typical of the *frum* world," she points out. "I became religious only in my 20s. I have a Ph.D. I've been divorced. I have only two children. I've been a career woman and a single mother, becoming a *rebbetzin* in my late 30s. And I've always followed my instincts. These facts all contribute to my self-confidence. I rarely feel any need or desire to conform."

Because she's clear about her identity and her spiritual needs, Rivkah doesn't mind being "out of the box." "I have to relate to God and Torah in a way that works for me," she states. "I don't practice Judaism based on someone else's idea of what it should look like. With input from various rabbis, I forge my own way. It may be idiosyncratic, but it's deeply gratifying. The only downside is that I'm sometimes something of a 'lonely woman of faith,' to paraphrase Rabbi

Joseph B. Soloveitchik. But I believe in what I'm doing, even if few others understand or follow along."

How does Rivkah's community respond to her unusual work? "Well, we just moved to Efrat, so that remains to be seen," she says. "But back in Ma'ale Adumim, I was actually given a fair amount of leeway, probably for two reasons. One, long before I got involved in teaching non-Jews Torah, I was contributing to my community, so my atypical occupation was seen as part of an overall positive package. Two, my husband was a respected rabbi who also gave a lot to the community. We're planning on being equally active in Efrat, so hopefully my work will be similarly accepted there.

"I do face opposition, though," Rivkah admits. "There are basically three kinds. The first comes from Jews who dismiss all Christians as missionaries trying to destroy Judaism. Many Christians do proselytize, of course. But the ones I teach have renounced Replacement Theology, the belief that Christianity replaced Judaism and that God no longer has a covenant with the Jewish people. Plenty of these non-Jews have paid dearly for following their souls, often losing friends, family, clergy, and congregations along the way. Their *mesirut nefesh* is inspiring.

"Many of my fellow Jews also question my teaching gentiles when there are so many woefully uneducated Jews. As I write in my book, however, Hashem keeps connecting me with non-Jews, so I believe this is the work He's asking me to do.

"The second kind of opposition comes from gentiles who suspect that *we're* trying to convert *them*. They're warned to stay away from us and regard us negatively, which is unfortunate.

"The third kind of opposition is internal. This is new territory, so the demarcation lines can be blurry. How can I reach out to other nations without crossing my own boundaries as a Torah-observant Jew? I constantly have to make my own beliefs clear to my students without getting pulled into discussing theirs. It's a challenge."

Rivkah's ultimate goal is to open an Israeli school where non-Jews can study Torah. "An estimated 22 million Christians are interested in exploring the Jewish roots of their faith," Rivkah says, "but very few Israeli institutions would welcome them, and generally only if they're considering conversion, which most aren't. That leaves online learning. The nations need Torah Jews to teach them in person, and in Israel.

"I envision a school where tourists could study for a day, a week, a month, or a year—or even drop in for a single lecture—focusing on the parts of Torah suitable for non-Jews. One day, there will be schools like this all over Israel, each with its own philosophy and attracting its own kind of student."

Meanwhile, Rivkah believes she's tapping the energy of the geulah, and she loves it. "I'm so blessed to be doing exactly what I'm cut out for. And Hashem is constantly opening doors for me, which gives me tremendous confidence.

"I'm doing my part to spread Torah to the world. The rest is in Hashem's hands."

> While students should be devoted to their teachers, they must independently develop their own powers of analysis and reach their own conclusions.* (Rabbi Yaakov Kamenetsky)

---

* There are obviously limits to independence, and it's important to consult a rabbi to check that one hasn't overstepped them.

Chapter Thirteen
Learning Curve

"[…] a new power has made itself felt in our lives. And every force that God sends into the world is meant to be used for holiness. Therefore, if God gave girls and women abstract abilities previously lacking, it was in order that they use them to learn Torah." — Devorah (Heshelis) Fastag, *The Moon's Lost Light*

RECHY KATZ* WAS born in 1987 to a Chassidic family, the oldest of 10 children.

"My father's parents were Holocaust survivors from Eastern Europe, devout *Chassidim* who eschewed secular education and embraced insularity," Rechy relates. "Upon immigrating to the U.S., however, many such Jews wanted college degrees and financial success for their children. But my father and his friends chose to follow in their grandparents' footsteps and adopt an insular lifestyle. My mother was

---

* Name and identifying characteristics have been changed.

a second-generation American but also from a Chassidic background.

"When my parents married, they joined a Chassidic enclave, a spiritual oasis in a sea of increasing materialism and superficiality. That's the world my parents wanted to give their children, and the world in which I was raised."

In many ways, Rechy was a typical kid. "I would dance with my sisters in the kitchen, loudly voice my opinions, and have lots of fun," she recalls. But Rechy was also exceptionally deep. "I was very sensitive and aware, always yearning for an emotional 'high.' I wanted to express my inner self but didn't know how."

Rechy had inherited her father's spiritual intensity, and she was highly intellectual as well. These traits put her at odds with her community's traditional female role.

"In the Chassidic world, women focus on the home," she says. "As nurturers and educators of their children, they're deeply respected. But their path to spirituality is very physical."

Rechy stood out in another way too. "Most young women in my community are light and cheerful. So intense thinkers like me are out of the box.

"In my teens, life became really challenging, because I was a misfit. I constantly felt different, weird, and wrong."

Fortunately, Rechy's parents were loving and tolerant, making room for their children to experiment and grow. Her father was also eager to share his spirituality.

"There are basically three types of fathers," Rechy observes. "The first thinks these strange little females are cute, but there's not much to do with them: 'One day she'll be a wife and mother. Meanwhile, let's just enjoy her.' The second sees girls as female boys, meaning they can't learn *Gemara* but should learn everything else. This approach works for a not terribly girly girl, but it imparts a deep sense that femininity isn't valuable. The third type of father gets his daughters' femininity and values and supports everything they are, including their minds."

Rechy's father encouraged his daughters to listen to tapes of Torah classes and even gave her one. From the first lecture, she was smitten. "It was electrifying," she remembers. "I'd never heard anything so powerful and intriguing."

Torah study soon became her life. "I drove my father nuts, begging him to get me every tape he could. Then I started buying them myself."

Rechy's learning transformed her. "My davening became deeply fulfilling, and I was incredibly happy," she says. "I had none of my schoolmates' issues and struggles. My heart and mind were so full!"

Rechy was particularly attracted to Chassidic teachings. "I gravitated toward *sefarim* that combine the esoteric and the philosophical, such as those of Rav Tzadok, Breslov, and Chabad. One of my favorite topics was the *sefirot*, the 10 attributes through which Hashem governs His world and shapes our personalities. I especially loved how the Chassidic masters were so positive, seeing goodness where others didn't."

But it wasn't easy being different. "My teachers were nice to me, but they didn't understand me," she says. "And a relative made fun of my intense prayer, so I avoided davening like that in public. I struggled not to feel ashamed.

"I was once pressured to go on a school trip that would have prevented me from learning and davening the way I wanted. I asked a *rav*, and he told me I couldn't live by other people's standards. That was a turning point."

Still, it took Rechy a while to feel comfortable with who she was. "At age 18, I asked that same *rav* whether the Torah dismissed female spiritual and intellectual achievement. He insisted that it didn't, that Judaism esteemed learned women, and that there was no reason I shouldn't be one. He gave me strength and encouragement. Eventually I learned to accept myself."

Chassidic girls marry young, but Rechy's parents worried about her marriageability—as did she. "There seems to be a feeling that intense, spiritual girls make bad wives, and I picked up on it," she says. "I was also different in totally superficial ways that apparently bother some people. For example, I wore shoes with shoelaces, because I found them more comfortable. Someone told me that my future mother-in-law would reject me for it."

Rechy and her parents had nothing to be concerned about—she met her husband, Shimon, when she was 18½. "One great gift of being *Chassidish* is that marriage is the default," she explains, "so if your parents are healthy and loving, they find you a great mate. Because I was so 'extreme' and 'intense,' I was paired with an equally extreme and intense young man. My mother-in-law, who's very similar to me, was thrilled. And she didn't even notice the shoelaces!"

The couple married on Rechy's 19th birthday. "I can't say my *chasan* and I knew each other very well," she admits. "But we each sensed that the other was a good, solid person, and that's what matters." Did Rechy's husband know what he was getting himself into? "We met only twice before we got engaged, for around an hour each time," she points out with a grin, "so you tell me."

Rechy had her first child at 20, and has since had several more. How does a woman so into abstract ideas deal with the very concrete mundanities of motherhood? "I wasn't prepared for the drudgery of diapers," Rechy acknowledges. "But as my husband and I matured together and faced the realities of parenthood, we learned how to incorporate life's more physical aspects.

"One benefit of a Torah lifestyle is that it encourages balance. It took an intellectual like me—who's accomplishment-oriented, craves structure, and lives on spiritual pursuits—and plunked her down in the middle of two toddlers and a newborn. That forced me to be loving, kind, and patient. I had to develop authority, learn to discipline, and set limits—and all the while having little opportunity to learn Torah or daven. It was unbelievably difficult. But it stretched me beyond anything I could imagine.

"Eventually I got the hang of it—I learned to set up routines, hire help, and carve out time for myself. In the process, I grew in ways I never knew I could.

"It's taken a good 10 years, but I've mostly worked through my challenges—though if you're looking for a preschool teacher, do NOT hire me!"

Like most young mothers in her community, Rechy works part-time but her day is full. "First I get the kids out, eat breakfast, daven, and straighten up. From 10 to 1, I transcribe and edit *shiurim* that various *rabbanim* have given me, which provides me with a deep sense of meaning and mission. From 1 to 3 I run errands, and from 3 to 10 I'm a mother again, with all the myriad tasks that entails, including making sure I hug all my children a lot. In the late evening, if I'm not collapsing, I talk to my budding teens.

"At the same time, I schedule pockets of time for learning. I tutor over the phone for Partners in Torah [an outreach organization] while doing housework. I also have a phone *chavrusa* every night.

"So that's what my day looks like. Of course, since I'm *Chassidish*, I can be an hour or two off schedule!"

Rechy no longer has the time she once did to go to shul. Thanks to her teenage sisters' babysitting, however, she gets there once in a while.

She and her husband don't have much time to really talk, but they laugh a lot.

Does he help at home? "As much as a man who works, learns, and davens three times a day can," Rechy says. "But I never 'waste' him on what some good household help can do. In the father department, he's great. And he's totally supportive of everything I am. He finds life with me a thrilling adventure!"

What has given Rechy the strength to go against the grain of her community? "I got it from my parents," she says. "My father and his friends had to fight their families and environment to be who they are. And my mother doesn't give a hoot what people think. She's always been open and accepting of all her children's *'meshugas'*—like when, at age 15, I decided to sew myself very 'original' clothes. So she took my passion for learning in stride. My parents figure that holiness is holiness, and goodness is goodness, so whatever works for you goes!

"Another critical support is my sister, 21 months younger than I, who's even more intense and intellectual than I am. We empty our brains out on each other, testing new ideas and processing our emotions in a kind of 'peer therapy.'

"But I get most of my strength from my soul, which simply demands satisfaction."

How does Rechy's community relate to her?

"It helps that I conform to my community's dress code, although I'm on the casual end of the spectrum, and I don't bother with matching outfits for my children. (I'm lucky they're dressed altogether!)

"Beyond that, I don't focus on how I'm different. I just live my life and work on finding common ground with others. That includes seeing *everyone* as 'different,' or special, because deep down, we all are. I've come to love people for who they are—and to humor them when necessary. At the same time, I've learned not to share all of myself with every person I meet, just with my closest friends."

Rechy's not the only one who's learned. "People have come to sense and appreciate my deep inner joy, even if they don't 'get' me," she says.

So she has no remaining struggles? Not quite. "At times I'm bothered by women's issues in the Torah," she says, "but thanks to Chassidic teachings, I'm coming to my own understanding of them."

I asked Rechy what learning Torah does for her, expecting a lofty, even rapturous response. Instead, she replied simply, "It makes me feel human—meaning, true to myself."

How does Rechy envision her future? "Well, God willing, I'd like to have more children, besides raising the holy little handful I already have. Growing up in a Chassidic enclave has given my kids a purity and a light in their eyes, and I'm looking forward to more of that. And, of course, I have the entire Torah to learn. I expect to be pretty busy."

> Look into your soul—have you revealed your true self? Are you a unique individual or just part of the human race? Differentiate. Reveal what makes you special. Become a person who chooses, and serve Hashem. (Piaseczner Rebbe)

Chapter Fourteen

The Call of the Open Road

FOR ANYONE MOVED by the great outdoors, it's a soul-stirring scene: A pickup truck and trailer parked in the middle of nowhere, dwarfed by pristine, snow-capped mountains and a magnificent glacier.

For over two and half years, sights such as these were routine for Ben and Tricia Wymore and their two children, as they followed "the call of the open road."

Ben was born in 1973 and Tricia in 1974, both to families with a deep appreciation for nature. Ben's parents had met in Los Angeles' Sierra Club and bequeathed their love of hiking and camping to their children. Ben learned about ecology, geology, and paleontology in summer camp and become an avid biker and kayaker. "For me, being outdoors was about more than nature—it was about exploration and discovery," he says. "My father always quoted Mallory's response to the question 'Why climb Everest?': 'Because it's there.'"

Ben's non-observant parents also tried to give their kids an appreciation of Judaism. When he was young, the family spent four years in Israel, and once back in California, Ben was enrolled in a Jewish day school. At age 9, however, his family moved to Hillsboro, Oregon, where his Jewish schooling ended. Although the family initially attended a Conservative synagogue every Friday night, Ben recalls that "my brother and I complained so much that my parents gave up on it, and we became the 'synagogue twice a year' types." His only remaining Jewish affiliation consisted of Sunday school, a small Young Judea group, and some disparate rituals. Nevertheless, his time in Israel—and the anti-Semitism he experienced as the only Jew in his high school—fostered a strong yet undefined Jewish identity.

Tricia, raised outside of Milwaukee, was a fellow nature-lover. At her parents' lakeside cottage, she spent many weekends surrounded by trees, swimming, boating, and fishing. Unlike Ben, however, she had no connection to Judaism.

By the time they reached college age, Ben and Tricia were each searching. "I never really knew the significance of being Jewish," Ben says, "but I wanted to find out." Tricia's quest was more open-ended. "Already in high school," she remembers, "I vowed to find a spiritual belief system—Jewish or not—that made sense to me." Upon entering Lawrence University in Appleton, Wisconsin, she enrolled in the first religion class that came her way. Fortunately, it was Judaism 101.

About a month into Tricia's freshman year, the two met on campus. "Ben was a speed roller skater, and I was a figure

skater and rollerblader," Tricia recalls. "I hadn't found anyone at college to skate with, and Ben couldn't find anyone
to match his pace. So one night around midnight, we skated
around town together. That was our first adventure!"

Once Ben discovered that Tricia was also interested in
learning about Judaism, they checked out Friday night services at Appleton's only synagogue, a Conservative congregation. Although nearly all the members were elderly men,
the couple enjoyed being there and continued attending
("we were the adopted grandchildren," Tricia jokes). They
even walked two and a half miles each way in the Wisconsin
winter out of respect for the rabbi, who was fairly observant,
and with whom they became close. Thus began four years of
slow but steady growth in Judaism—and in Ben and Tricia's
relationship.

On the morning of June 9, 1996, Tricia graduated. In the
evening, she and Ben were married.

The newlyweds moved to Minneapolis, where Ben had
begun a master's in computer science. To maintain their
Shabbat observance, they chose an apartment inside the
eruv of the Orthodox community. The large Conservative
synagogue in town felt too impersonal, but the small Orthodox shul was welcoming, and Ben soon befriended the rabbi, with whom he started learning. He even taught biology
in the local Bais Yaakov. Naturally, the couple's observance
increased.

When Ben completed his degree, he and Tricia celebrated in the best way they could think of. Ben put together a
bicycle built for two, and in the summer of 1997, the couple
hit the road. Starting in Yorktown, Virginia, they hoped to
bike the TransAmerica Trail. They began cycling through

Virginia, visiting historic sites and camping out at night. But after a crash on the Virginia-Kentucky border left them stranded and awaiting parts, they'd had enough. Yet their tendency to dream big would serve them well, and this two-week trip hinted at greater things to come.

The Wymores moved back to Ben's hometown, where he began working for Intel. Always looking to deepen their Judaism, they checked out the Orthodox synagogue in Portland. The rabbi and his wife turned out to be wonderfully warm and very skilled in *kiruv*. Under their kind and patient mentorship, Ben and Tricia blossomed religiously. Gradually, they became fully *shomer Shabbat*.

Thanks to their connection with the small Portland community, the Wymores purchased their first RV. "We wanted to go to shul on Shabbos," Ben recounts, "but because Trish was running a preschool from our brand-new, 2,000-square-foot house in the suburbs, moving didn't feel like an option. So we bought an RV, towed it half an hour to Portland, and parked it at the shul on *erev Shabbos*. We slept in the camper over Shabbos, then towed it home afterward." Thus began Ben and Tricia's acquaintance with RV "travel."

Over the next few years, Ben and Tricia transitioned to full religious observance. Since their first wedding was halachically questionable, they renewed their commitment to each other in an Orthodox ceremony attended by the whole Portland community. Their new marriage put a public stamp on years of personal spiritual growth.

Not long afterward, Tricia flew to Israel to study at Neve Yerushalayim for a few weeks to further solidify her own religiosity. "I had been struggling with covering my hair," she relates. "But I came home wearing a *sheitel!*"

Ben and Tricia began taking their RV to the beach and the mountains. "We loved going places with our own little 'kosher hotel,'" Ben says. At the same time, they grew closer to their community. Eventually, that connection trumped their enthusiasm for RV travel. Realizing the importance of living near their friends, attending daily minyanim, and hosting Shabbat guests, they sold their house and RV and rented the townhouse next door to their rabbi.

In 2001 their oldest son, Mechel, was born. Having a child made them think seriously about their future, and they considered relocating to a larger community. "Ben and I wanted more *frum* role models," Tricia recounts. Adds Ben, "Our rabbi had suggested that I go to yeshivah, and there wasn't one in Portland. On the other hand, I had this great job, and it seemed crazy to leave." In the end, he didn't have to. A few months later, Intel canceled his project, and he was given six months' severance pay. "Hashem was clearly giving us a nudge," Tricia says.

The couple moved to the religious community of Monsey, New York. Ben's severance package funded a year of study for him at the local branch of Yeshivat Ohr Somayach.

In 2004 their daughter Baila was born. Yet even two small children couldn't keep the Wymores from doing what they loved most. "We started hiking and backpacking with Mechel as soon as he could sit up," Tricia recollects. "When Baila was born, we bought a second child carrier, so we could 'wear' both kids as we hiked. We took them snowshoeing as early as they could manage. And when they were 4 and 2, we kayaked overnight down the Delaware River."

By the time Baila was 6, her parents had bought another RV, traveling whenever they could.

Religiously grounded, with two children who were already seasoned outdoorspeople, these happy campers were ready for their greatest adventure.

In 2012, Ben and Tricia began entertaining a daring notion that would take their love of RV travel to a whole new level: a year-long family road trip. It would mean not only leaving their jobs but homeschooling their kids. Excited, they shared the idea with their community. The reaction was less than positive. "We encountered lots of skepticism and very little encouragement," Ben recounts. "Mostly, we were warned that our kids would be socially deprived, their growth stunted, and they'd later have trouble with *shidduchim*. And although people didn't say so, I sensed they were concerned about our Yiddishkeit." The negative feedback was so overwhelming, it almost convinced them not to go.

In the end, however, Ben and Tricia were undeterred. "We discussed the potential risks and issues with our rabbi," Ben relates. "We also listed all the reasons we should embark on this once-in-a-lifetime journey. One reason was 'stuff.' We realized that owning stuff was one big waste of time—from the time spent earning money to buy it to the time spent maintaining, storing, and ultimately disposing of it. RV living would be simpler and less distracting from the important things in life."

Furthermore, says Ben, "I was out all day making money to pay other people to educate our children. So I figured, why not skip the work, live on less, and teach the kids ourselves?"

But the couple had an even more significant reason for taking their trip: to give Mechel and Baila a profound appreciation of God's world. "We wanted them to see as much as possible of North America's natural beauty," Tricia explains. "We knew it would be an incredible experience for them—and for the family."

Ben remodeled their RV to allow for more comfortable long-term living and homeschooling (or "road-schooling," as RVers call it). He installed rooftop solar panels and a large water tank. He and Tricia quit their jobs and rented out their house, so they could live off the income. Finally, Ben created a website and blog, "so my mother wouldn't worry too much," and so others could share in the trek.

On August 8, 2013, with Mechel going into seventh grade and Baila into fourth—and just as Tricia became a certified Montessori teacher—the family took off, with four kayaks atop their SUV and four bicycles strapped to the back of their travel trailer.

The Wymores headed straight to one of America's most beautiful places, Yosemite National Park in California, arriving 12 days later. They spent over a week among its breathtaking mountains, trees, and lakes. As Rosh HaShanah approached, they traveled up to Portland for the holidays. They then went south for the winter, slowly making their way down the stunning coast of Oregon and northern California. "We spent a week camped near an amazing little stretch of beach, and the kids built an entire pirate ship out of driftwood," Tricia reminisces. "That was a magical time!"

Although the Wymores had intended to be on the road for a year, after only eight months they knew they wanted more. In April 2014 they exchanged their SUV for a pickup truck and their travel trailer for a much larger (and, being new, conveniently kosher for Passover) fifth-wheel RV. With their relatively spacious new accommodations, they headed

north to the wilds of Alaska for the summer. Ben's auto re-
pair skills were tested when a broken axle pin stranded them
on a dirt road in the Yukon, 150 miles from the nearest parts
store. Nevertheless, our fearless travelers made it all the way
to the Arctic Ocean on Alaska's northern coast (though they
chose not to jump into its icy waters).

In September, the family drove south to Henderson, Ne-
vada, where Ben's parents now lived, to celebrate Mechel's
bar mitzvah. The Wymores spent the winter of 2015 in the
Desert Southwest, followed by spring in Utah. They then
headed back east so Tricia and Baila could ride 60 miles
in Chai Lifeline's Tour de Simcha bike-a-thon (not yet bat
mitzvah, Baila was the youngest participant). For the summer, they went north to Nova Scotia.

The Wymores had now been on the road for two years.
But it still wasn't enough. Once more, they extended their

trip and headed west. Tricia can't even remember all the places they visited. "I think we went to Texas, and I know we went to Florida, but I forget exactly when. I'm so glad we took tons of photographs and kept a detailed travel log to jog our memory!"

The family spent many Shabbatot and *chagim* in Jewish communities across America, even hosting others. Tricia wishes she'd had room for more than two guests at a time (although given that she had exactly one pot and pan each for meat and dairy, it's impressive that she fed even her own family). Sometimes, however, Shabbat found the Wymores far from civilization. "One *erev Shabbos* in Utah, we camped in an alpine meadow directly across from the Grand Tetons," Tricia recalls. "The view took my breath away—it was the most amazing place we'd ever davened on Shabbos. When facing something that majestic, it's impossible not to feel the grandeur of Hashem and His creation." (Her words remind me of a bumper sticker I once saw: "See Nature—Think God.")

Aside from their homeschooling schedule, the Wymores basically came and went as they pleased. "We generally stayed put four days a week, so the kids could study," Tricia explains. "They'd be 'in school' in the mornings, and in the afternoons we'd often hike. The rest of the week, we'd go wherever and do whatever we wanted."

It sounds so idyllic: a radiant family happily bouncing along the trail, reveling in the wonders of nature. But what was it really like taking the kids on all those hikes—never mind spending nearly 24 hours a day together?

"Mechel and Baila were like any other pre-teens—alternatively hilarious and irritating," Tricia says. "It took us about three months to get used to being in such close quarters with them.

"They were great hikers, but that didn't stop them from complaining. Our first outing was for three days in Yosemite, where we trekked seven miles uphill to Young Lakes. The kids had their own backpacks, and it was hot and difficult. Sometimes they wanted to give up. But they persevered. They learned resilience, and we learned to work as a team.

"The whole trip was like that. Baila and Mechel probably would have gone to amusement parks every day! But we nudged them out of their comfort zone, and they usually had a great time. Sometimes it was hard, but sometimes it was incredible. Most days it was both. On the whole, the trip was absolutely wonderful."

All in all, in two years and eight months, the Wymores passed through 47 states, 40 out 60 U.S. national parks (including 160-plus park sites), as well as Mexico and Canada. "We climbed sand dunes and glaciers, walked beneath the world's tallest trees, and panned for gold in the Yukon Territory beneath the midnight sun," Ben recounts. "Personally, I got to bicycle many of the toughest cycling climbs in the U.S. I also realized my long-time dream of owning and flying a powered paraglider, from which you see everything from a beautiful new perspective. In the meantime, our children grew up so much in so many ways. And we became closer as a family."

By the end of the winter of 2016, Tricia felt the need for "normal" life again. While Ben could have continued traveling, he too realized the time had come to go home. "It was mostly about Mechel," he explains. "He was now a full-fledged teenager, and he needed to be in yeshivah, learning *Gemara* with experienced rabbis and making friends."

So on April 17, 2016, after 984 days on the road, the Wymores finally returned home.

Their reception was very different from their send-off. What had changed?

For one thing, *Ami* magazine had run a very positive article about their adventures, which garnered enthusiastic reader responses. One person wrote, "In our fast-paced world, we often miss what Hashem's world can show us. The vast beauty of unspoiled landscapes and the hidden treasures of our national parks are something we should all take time out to explore and enjoy. If we love Hashem's world, isn't that a *kiyum* of *'ve'ahavta es Hashem Elokecha'* [and you shall love the Lord, your God]?" Another commented, "It was such a refreshing read and a good reminder that there are different strokes for different folks."

Yet Ben hopes that article wasn't the only reason his family was welcomed back. "What, we're okay now just because *Ami* says so?" he quips. Ben offers another theory: "When everyone saw we were still *frum* and our kids were thriving, I think that also changed people's minds."

All those months out west left Ben and Tricia yearning to live there again. They decided to move—but for some strange reason, their house wasn't selling. Realizing they might be getting another sign from God, they decided to stay put.

"While there are wonderful *frum* communities all over the U.S., Monsey is special," Ben says. "Here, it's Shabbos even outside, whereas almost anywhere else, we'd be walking past our neighbor washing his car. There are tons of religious kids for our children to befriend. Maybe most important, we live in a neighborhood with serious learners who have inspired us to continue growing in our Yiddishkeit."

Adds Tricia, "We also realized that, not having *frum* parents or siblings, our neighbors and friends in Monsey had become our family. And we knew we'd need a strong support system to get through the teenage years!"

While waiting for their tenants to move out, the Wymores continued living in their RV—parked in their driveway—for almost two months. By now, the family was used to it.

Today, the Wymores are once again living normal, suburban lives (although Tricia jokes that going from one part of her house to another feels like a workout!). But they still keep it simple. They even sold all the "stuff" they'd put in storage.

Needless to say, the family continues to travel whenever possible, including long summer trips and shorter ones throughout the year. The Wymores have repeatedly visited Assateague Island, off the Maryland coast, to see the wild horses. In the summer of 2017, the family took off for four weeks to view the solar eclipse as it trailed across the United States—the first viewable eclipse in North America since 1979, and the first whose visibility spanned the country since 1918. And in the summer of 2018, always seeking new ways to experience the outdoors, they drove their RV coast to coast with sport motorcycles in tow.

Back at home, the Wymores make do with local outdoor activities. "I take friends out on the tandem bicycle Trish and I rode across Virginia back in 1997," Ben says. "We also take people kayaking with our little flotilla. And we putter on the Hudson River in our ancient speedboat, though we don't take it down to the park on *Chol HaMoed* anymore, because literally hundreds of *Chassidim* stop and stare."

Both Ben and Tricia hope for many more travels. "Once the kids are married, my ideal life would be 'motor home to nursing home,'" Ben jokes. "With just the two of us, we can use an itinerant lifestyle not just to see new places, but to help out in far-flung Jewish communities and do *chesed* projects." Tricia is totally on board.

How have Ben and Tricia managed to stay so "out of the box" despite social pressure? "We've always had a 'can-do' attitude," says Ben. "Back in college, when we learned we were supposed to have a second Pesach seder, which our Conservative rabbi didn't do, we made our own. Contrast this with people raised religious who've always gone to their parents' or in-laws' for Pesach and are anxious about making their first seder in their 40s! Having to do for yourself builds self-confidence and allows you to follow your own path."

Tricia adds, "Only after moving to a large religious town did I realize boxes existed altogether! I spent the next 15 years trying to fit into some of them, rejecting others, and ultimately accepting myself and continuing to grow in my own box."

Though they've stayed true to themselves, the Wymores strongly affiliate with their more conventional community. "We've found friends who come from backgrounds and experiences similar to ours, or who simply value who we are and don't care what weird things we do," Tricia says. "I sing in a *frum* women's choir, teach girls' gymnastics in a *frum* gym, and daven in a shul I love. I feel very connected to the people around me. Most of the time, I don't even realize we're different."

Ben, however, acknowledges the challenge in negotiating individuality within community. "There's a fascinating tension in the *frum* world between being true to oneself and being part of *Klal Yisrael*," he points out. "As a result, many people are afraid of being different, of being judged by their neighbors. Maybe I should have that fear, but I don't. I check in with my rabbi, then ask myself, 'Am I making a *kiddush Hashem?*' People will judge or not, approve or not."

Tricia concurs. "Hashem gave me an absolutely unique path to Him, so I'm pretty certain He doesn't want me to be just like everyone else. While I'd like our kids to have a fairly normative religious upbringing, I'm always trying to understand what Hashem wants from me and how I can come close to Him in my own way."

Ben considers their 984 days on the road the most transformative chapter of their lives. "If you think about daily family interactions," Ben says, "a lot is 'Do, do, do,' or 'Go, go, go.' It's 'Get up, get dressed, go to school, hurry, we have to be on time.' Traveling removed all that pressure.

"But our trip did more than that. Abandoning most of our possessions and spending so much time with our family was amazing. There was a certain purity about it. In retrospect, it was almost a spiritual act.

"We had hoped to have time together, to experience America's natural wonders, to teach and learn from our children, and to get to know each other better. We wanted to explore, dream, and discover. And we did."

> Fundraising would be much easier if I didn't wear Chassidic garb. But what can I do? This is who I am! If I dressed differently, it would be dishonest. (Rabbi Shlomo Freifeld)

Chapter Fifteen
The Obstacle is the Path

PEOPLE RESPOND TO difficult childhoods in different ways. Some who experienced trauma struggle indefinitely with the aftermath, while others move past it and even assist fellow victims. Some who were abused become or marry abusers, while others enter into healthy, happy marriages and educate the public about abuse. Many factors determine how someone emerges from a painful upbringing.

Devorah Horowitz* was raised in a dysfunctional family. Yet she rose above her circumstances and has made it her life's work to help others heal as she has.

The oldest of seven children, Devorah grew up in an ultra-Orthodox home that seemed picture-perfect—from the outside. "My childhood was hell," she recounts. "My mother

---

* Name and other details have been changed to protect her privacy.

would tease me and yell constantly. My father, a control freak, tried manipulating my siblings and me into following his every whim and verbally assaulted anyone who didn't. He also overstepped bounds with endless inappropriate, often sexual comments.

"Life was very confusing. When we had company, my parents were nice, but afterward, they were mean again. I invited friends over as a safety net. I felt so helpless and alone. I knew we were supposed to pretend and cover up, but I also knew something about that was very wrong."

Although Devorah was often sad, she had numerous strengths. She was bright, musically gifted, and athletic. Furthermore, she had an uncanny ability to pick up on people's feelings—as do many whose well-being depends on others' moods. "As early as third grade, I would sit for hours analyzing the world around me," she recalls. "I watched people closely and learned a lot about human behavior. Reading my childhood diary, I'm surprised at the depth of my observations."

Devorah attended an elementary school whose students were generally, like her, well-to-do. But she craved a less materialistic, more "authentic" environment. So she chose a high school catering mostly to simple, Chassidic families with little money. "I once went to a classmate's home and saw small holes in the wall, chipped paint, and a fridge containing the bare minimum," Devorah remembers. "I was afraid to invite her to my house, because I was embarrassed to be so different." Happily, her new friends didn't care about her background, and she flourished in their company. Finally she felt at home.

Then, at age 14, came the first bombshell. Devorah learned that two of her sisters had been molested for months by an uncle. The fact is, Devorah had also been victimized (along with two cousins). When she was little, this same uncle had bullied her into viewing pornography. After her sisters' story came out, she told her parents her own. They warned the uncle not to go near their daughters again, but that was all. "I begged my parents to get him locked up and to send my sisters and me to therapy," says Devorah. "Their reaction was: 'Therapy is for crazies. It will mess you up and ruin your chances in *shidduchim*.' They were terribly afraid of the stigma. So they never reported the abuse to the police. And we were forbidden to discuss it."

By the time Devorah was 15, her family life was taking its toll. She suffered from anxiety, nightmares, and bouts of sobbing. She knew she had to address her pain, but that her parents would never pay for counseling. So she worked evenings and Sundays for just over minimum wage, saving every penny for therapy. At last, she hoped, she was on the road to recovery. Yet she couldn't find a therapist who could really help her.

A few months later, Devorah hit bottom. "I was crying hysterically in the bathroom," she remembers. "I just couldn't take it anymore. I had to get out." Fortunately, a warm and loving family she knew offered to take her in. She packed a large suitcase, dropped it from the balcony to the garden, and slipped out the door.

For the next two and a half years, Devorah lived with this family, commuting two hours to and from school every day. Even her closest friends knew nothing about her living arrangements. Travel was expensive, and because the earliest bus still got her to school after the bell, she had to sit detention weekly *and* pay late fees daily. To come up with the money, she worked ten hours every Sunday.

Devorah's adopted family connected her with a Jewish psychologist specializing in trauma. Although the process was difficult, slowly but surely, she began to heal. "Initially, I struggled tremendously with the idea of being counseled by someone who wasn't Torah-observant," Devorah recounts. "But the change she helped bring about was incredible. Therapy with her was the greatest gift I've ever given myself."

Meanwhile, more bombshells were falling. "Shortly after leaving home, I met someone my age who almost died from an eating disorder," Devorah relates. "Her parents had to fight for her life.

"Then, a few months later, a camp friend told me she'd been sexually abused by her brother. Then an acquaintance revealed that her father's addiction to alcohol and gambling was destroying the family. Then *another* person confided in me that her parents beat her. In all these cases, everything was hushed up, the victims were full of secrecy and shame, and they weren't getting help. I said to myself, 'This is crazy! Someone has to do something!'"

At the time, Devorah was discovering what proper psychological help can do. "I understood that pain like mine doesn't just go away unless you address it," she says. "I experienced the power of healing that Hashem put into the world through psychology, and it was amazing. I began to feel I had a mission to help others as I'd been helped." Despite her insular, ultra-Orthodox background, she decided to pursue a Ph.D. in psychology.

During her post–high school year in an Israeli Bais Yaakov seminary (which she attended on scholarship), Devorah
started planning her academic future. As expected, her principal and teachers were adamantly opposed. "They were
very against secular education, particularly in the field of
psychology, which includes values antithetical to Torah," she
recalls. "They said it was dangerous and could lead a person
to stop being religious. I was warned again and again that
nothing good could ever come from *kefirah* and that studying psychology was an *issur d'oraisa* with dire consequences."

Devorah actually sympathized with these educators. "I
was a straight-A student, and they had high hopes for me,"
she says. "They were right to make me aware of the very real
challenges I'd be facing."

To be sure she was doing the right thing, Devorah consulted two world-renowned Israeli rabbis. Seeing how
strong she was religiously, and how noble her motivations—
and knowing how important it was that there be female Orthodox psychologists—both backed her decision.

When it came time to start her bachelor's degree, however, Devorah got cold feet. No one she knew was attending a
secular college, and it was difficult for her to imagine doing
so. Instead, she and a seminary friend enrolled in a religious
program popular in the *yeshivish* community and offering a
general science degree. But Devorah soon realized that this
diploma wouldn't get her into a top-tiered graduate school.
So she switched to a reputable private college, where she
took a slew of psychology classes and engaged in research in
order to become eligible for a Ph.D. program.

Meanwhile, an American rabbi well-versed in mental health became her guide. "Toward the end of my

undergraduate studies, I had a long talk with this *rav*," Devorah tells me. "He assured me that he was available to discuss any questions that arose in grad school. He also put me in touch with a religious, female social worker who would serve as my *hashkafic* mentor. We agreed that if either one of them felt my *frumkeit* was suffering, I would quit school immediately."

To get the best training, Devorah applied to programs so competitive that hundreds apply but only a handful are admitted. Yet she was accepted to such top-notch universities as Yale and Stanford. How? "I made a lot of connections in the college world, plus I worked very hard," she says. "But that doesn't really explain it. Bottom line, it happened because Hashem wanted it for me."

As a doctoral candidate, Devorah excelled and thrived. She conducted high level research, presented at international conferences, published in respected journals, and won honors, awards, and fellowships. She also started a small mentoring group in her community, guiding Jewish girls through abusive or other difficult family situations. "Most of these victims are no longer *frum*, because they were told to keep quiet," she reports sadly. "I witnessed the pain and shame they suffered in silent isolation. And I learned that emotional dysfunction is caused not necessarily by abuse, but by lack of support. When victims finally find the courage to seek help—whether from a therapist, a support group, or an organization—a positive response is crucial."

Passionate about helping such people, Devorah decided to specialize in trauma under the mentorship of two internationally renowned psychologists. She studied the latest treatment models and contributed to research in the field.

Throughout her intensive six-year Ph.D. program, Devorah continued to receive well-intentioned rebuke for her chosen path. "I took people's criticism very seriously," she says. "It was a great *nisayon* to be in a secular environment so many hours a day, in the constant company of people from backgrounds vastly different from mine. In addition, because not all the material presented in my classes and textbooks accorded with Torah, I had to filter it. I had to be super-vigilant in order to maintain my Torah standards. So although the reproof was unpleasant at times, I always thanked my critics for helping me keep my head in the right place. Nevertheless, I reiterated that I would quit only if my *rav* or mentor told me I should. Thankfully, neither one did."

Since leaving home at age 16, Devorah hadn't received any financial support from her parents. "But *HaKadosh Baruch Hu* was with me every step of the way," she is quick to add. She held various jobs, from tutoring and babysitting to secretarial and lab work. A research company hired her to write scientific manuscripts. Small scholarships helped pay her tuition. And she boarded with a kindhearted family who let her pay whatever she could. "They lived simply but happily," Devorah tells me. "I had a teeny bedroom in their unfinished attic—the size of my mother's walk-in closet—with low, sloped ceilings. It was often cold, and I slept on a tilted mattress, because the floor was slanted. But they were so wonderful and loving, and taught me so much through example, that I wouldn't have lived anywhere else. Every day with them was a gift."

Devorah's siblings, with whom she is very close, were proud of her decision to pursue a Ph.D. and visited her often. Her friends from high school and seminary couldn't relate to what she was doing but were remarkably supportive. Her parents' reaction was more complicated.

"Initially, they were very opposed and cynical," Devorah relates. "Given that I was learning how to treat abuse, I understand why they felt threatened. Over the years, their negativity slowly decreased. At this point, we're back in phone contact, and the relationship is healthier. At the same time, getting married and having a family of my own, plus moving to a different city, has made it easy to maintain a healthy distance.

"I've also acquired many psychological skills that help me interact with my parents," she elaborates. "I've learned to focus on what they have rather than everything they're lacking; to recognize their shortcomings without being terrified of their behavior; to feel sympathetic rather than intimidated; and to communicate with them effectively while maintaining healthy boundaries.

"You can't force someone else to change—you can only change yourself and how you deal with others. So rather than nurturing unrealistic expectations, I've focused on my side of the relationship, including a lot of *tefillah*. Once I gave up on my dream of a close relationship with emotionally healthy parents and instead worked on myself, I saw tremendous improvement."

Devorah currently runs a busy private practice within the *yeshivish* and Chassidic communities. "I'm grateful that I can treat Yiddish-speakers," she says, "as few practitioners within the *Chassidish* community have advanced training in trauma. I'm also finishing a seven-year research project. The data will be used to develop a new program for survivors of abuse. I want the many psychotherapists in our community to have access to this latest study, and I'll be training them, so they won't need to go outside the community, as I did.

"Once I start disseminating my findings and protesting the silence that too often prevails, I may encounter resistance, as *frum* women are rarely vocal about such sensitive topics. But with the guidance of my *rav*, I intend to stand up and make a difference."

What helped Devorah transcend her abusive background and become who she is today? She lists several "protective factors," as psychologists call them. "I never felt trapped or hopeless—I always knew I could leave my situation and get help," she reflects. "I had great friends, a wonderful aunt, and a deeply loving connection with my grandfather, my spiritual mentor. My 'safe family' supported me throughout my journey, and so did my siblings, which shielded me from shame and guilt. My life was never threatened, and I was never beaten or sexually assaulted. And I attended to my trauma symptoms before they became severe."

Devorah also credits her faith and trust in God. Indeed, religious belief has been proven to contribute to healing. "My Yiddishkeit has been at the core of my recovery," Devorah states. "I believe Hashem gives us each *nisyonos* but also the ability to choose our responses. My grandfather, who suffered the *gehinnom* of the concentration camps, always told me that Hashem loves us and that all pain serves a purpose. I cling to my faith and use it to uplift myself and others.

Knowing Hashem believes in me has enabled me to believe in myself."

Yet Devorah notes that faith alone won't necessarily heal victims of abuse or other trauma. "While faith is crucial to healing and to living a fulfilling life while suffering, it doesn't guarantee that the pain will go away," she stresses. "But it does give our suffering meaning by telling us that there's a bigger picture and a future. Belief in a loving God can also help fill the emotional void that many abuse survivors feel."

Has anything changed in the treatment of abuse since Devorah's ordeal? "There's now a wonderful organization, Amudim, which I wish had been around when I was a teenager," she tells me. "They run workshops to raise awareness about abuse and addiction, provide guidance and emotional support to anyone who calls, and fund therapy for minors who've been sexually assaulted. Amudim has helped many people recover. They also train rabbis, educators, and camp counselors to recognize and address signs of abuse. When I was living away from home, coming late to high school every day and falling asleep at my desk, it didn't occur to my teachers to ask me if something was wrong. Today they probably would. Thanks to Amudim, victims are now more likely to be identified and get the help they need."

Devorah admits her upbringing has scarred her. She still jumps anytime something breaks, because she automatically expects yelling. But she's learned to recognize these and other "triggers" and counteract the emotions they arouse.

Devorah is now happily raising her two children and supporting her husband, who is learning in *kollel*. "I haven't taken the typical path for an ultra-Orthodox girl," she acknowledges. "*Shidduchim* were hard, and it took me a while to find the right man. People kept telling me, 'Men won't want to marry you with that degree.' I would reply, 'I'm sure one will, and that's all I need!' Not only did my husband not mind my Ph.D., but he staunchly supports my work and has added tremendous joy to my life and mission.

"Experience has taught me that I can overcome difficult situations and make a difference in others' lives. My message to those who're struggling is twofold: Suffering has a purpose, and there are resources for healing. If one path doesn't work, keep looking. Build from your pain, and you'll transcend it. Believe in yourself. Most important, never give up."

> Abraham served Hashem based on a consciousness of his singularity and uniqueness. He didn't let society prevent him from doing what he believed in. Neither should we.
> (Rabbi Nachman of Breslov)

Chapter Sixteen
A Brooklyn Girl Changing Israel

MOST WOMEN'S LIVES are complex. Like the moon, they go through phases: singlehood, wifehood, motherhood, career, etc. Each phase has its challenges—and its opportunities.

Rachel Levmore's life is a striking example. Only after having seven children and approaching middle age did she reach unprecedented heights in women's Torah study and become an activist to whom many women owe their lives. Yet Rachel sees herself as "just a girl from Brooklyn."

Rachel's European father emigrated to Palestine in the 1930s, while her mother survived the horrors of the Holocaust. The two met after the war in the newly created State of Israel, married, and later immigrated to the U.S. In 1954, they were blessed with their only child, Rachel, named after her father's sister, who was murdered by the Nazis.

Torah is in Rachel's blood, with such illustrious ancestors as the Bible and Talmud commentator Rabbi Solomon Itzhaki (better known as Rashi), mystic and philosopher Rabbi Judah Loew of Prague (Maharal), and Mishnah commentator Rabbi Yom Tov Lippman Heller (the *Tosfot Yom Tov*). Her family tree also featured at least one erudite woman, her great-grandmother. After the passing of her husband, a rabbinic judge, people submitted their questions to her.

Rachel grew up in a multicultural Jewish environment in Brooklyn, surrounded by European Chassidic aunts and uncles as well as American neighbors. Her family prayed in a variety of venues, from *shtiebelach* to Modern Orthodox synagogues. Yiddish was spoken at home when she was young, and both the Holocaust and love of Israel were ever-present.

Rachel's parents had high hopes for her, enrolling her in the best Jewish day schools, and she in turn excelled. She was the first from her high school and social circle to spend a year at the Michlalah seminary in Jerusalem, where she studied in both the American and Israeli programs. Upon returning to the U.S., Rachel majored in chemistry at Brooklyn College. Throughout, she read without end.

A product of the Bnei Akiva youth movement, Rachel was an ardent Zionist. "I had a burning desire to live in Israel and felt alienated from New York life," she relates. Rachel spent a few summers in Israel with relatives and couldn't wait to return for good. After marrying at age 20, graduating college, and having her first child, she promptly made *aliyah* with her husband. They moved from kibbutz to town to moshav before settling in Efrat, a new religious Zionist community in Gush Etzion (the Eztion Bloc), outside Jerusalem, which they helped establish. "Living in Gush Etzion strengthens one's character," Rachel says. "You're surrounded by Jewish history while continuing to make that history." Indeed, she was to make more history than she anticipated.

Rachel raised her family while helping her husband in business. She also initiated high-level Torah classes for women, whom she encouraged to speak at community celebrations. Most important, she never stopped learning Torah.

At age 38, when her youngest was 4, Rachel wanted to take her Torah study to a new level. Her timing couldn't have been better: Ohr Torah Stone Institutions had recently established a groundbreaking program training women to advocate in rabbinic courts. Rachel took the plunge and enrolled.

"Growing up, I had no idea that society had different expectations for men and women," Rachel tells me. "I was also very idealistic; I just did what felt right. As I matured, that meant sometimes doing things women traditionally didn't do. Joining this program, however, was much bigger. I had to muster up courage to go where women had never gone.

"In addition to the intellectual and spiritual challenge, this training would let me use my love of Torah to assist those in my community, who often turned to me for help. I thought: If I don't do this, who will?

"But there was another reason I wanted to do the program. My mother's father, Rabbi Mordechai Rosen, of blessed memory, headed a rabbinic court in Vienna. As such, he was one of the first Viennese Jews murdered by the Nazis, *yimach shemam*. I wanted to continue his life's work, which was cut short."

A rabbinic court advocate (*to'enet rabbanit* in Hebrew) is essentially a lawyer of Jewish law and usually handles divorces. Many women in these cases prefer female advocates, with whom they can more readily discuss intimate marital issues. "Many times a woman wants a divorce because of what is or isn't going on in the bedroom," Rachel points out. "Most women, especially in the religious community, won't tell a man the entire story. As a result, he won't represent her properly in court, and the judges will rule without knowing all the facts. That's not justice."

Rachel's training proved every bit as rigorous as she'd hoped. "It was sink or swim in the sea of halachah," she recalls. "We had to catch up to men who'd been studying full-time their entire lives."

An overachiever, Rachel went above and beyond the program requirements. "My *chavruta* and I delved very deep," she recounts. "We reached the point where we not only thoroughly understood the law, but gained insight into the very process of rendering a legal ruling, which even rabbinical students don't typically learn."

Finally, after three years of intensive study, the women were ready to be tested.

"To become licensed, we had to pass not only the exams in the program itself," Rachel explains, "but also those administered by the Israeli Chief Rabbinate. After that, we were tested orally by three judges. It was quite an ordeal."

Since female advocates were a new phenomenon, it took some time and effort—including an appeal to the Supreme Court—before Rachel and her classmates were allowed to take the exams. Rachel passed with flying colors, and in 1996, the Chief Rabbi of the High Rabbinical Court signed her license. Rachel had arrived. But this was only the beginning.

Throughout her adult life, but particularly toward the end of her studies, Rachel had been painfully aware of the *agunah* ("chained woman")* problem. In Jewish law, divorce is effected when the husband gives his wife a *get*, a bill of divorce, and she accepts it. Mutual consent is required, and either party can refuse. However, it is usually men—often with personality disorders or other emotional issues—who engage in the power play of denying their wives a *get*. Some husbands simply disappear. The wife is then left an *agunah*, "chained" in a defunct yet still legally binding marriage.

Rachel resolved to ease the plight of these *agunot*. As she expected, it wasn't easy. "Every time a new woman would come to me with her story, my heart sank," Rachel remembers. "An *agunah* lives in deep emotional, spiritual, and existential pain. I couldn't help but share that pain, as well as her tremendous frustration and anger at her husband's manipulative behavior. But I had to rise above that and use my knowledge of halachah and understanding of human nature to help her, along with my experience, creativity, and often chutzpah. I had to formulate a cool-headed plan of action. I could do that time after time only because I knew I was acting justly and in complete accordance with halachah."

Rachel represented *agunah* after *agunah*, convincing the court to order these husbands to divorce their wives. Having

---

* Technically, this term refers only to women whose husbands have disappeared in war, at sea, etc. Colloquially, however, it also includes women whose husbands refuse to grant them a divorce.

embarked upon a career historically reserved for men, she sometimes encountered disrespect from her male coworkers. "Fortunately," she says with a smile, "that usually dissipated after the judges ruled in my favor."

Needless to say, Rachel's successes made everything worthwhile. How does it feel to help free an *agunah*? "I experience tremendous satisfaction, of course, but much more than that. Relief. Exhilaration. Tears of joy."

A year after receiving her license, Rachel began working on a master's degree in Talmud at Bar Ilan University. Writing a thesis was way out of her comfort zone, but she rose to the occasion and graduated *summa cum laude*. Her thesis dealt with *get* refusal and its prevention through halachic prenuptial agreements.

The Rabbinical Council of America had formulated a powerful prenup years earlier, and Rachel was determined to introduce one in Israel too. In order for such a document to stand up in religious *and* civil courts, she and her rabbinic colleagues consulted both rabbinic and civil judges as well as lawyers. The resulting "Agreement for Mutual Respect" was published in 2000. Egalitarian in nature, it was designed to prevent a husband from refusing to grant a divorce *and* a wife from refusing to accept one. According to Rachel, this prenup has been 100% effective in eliminating *get* refusal.

That same year, Rachel became the only woman ever appointed to the Israeli rabbinic courts' *Agunah* Unit. While her new position precluded her working in private practice, it allowed her to "go behind the scenes" and assist *agunot* that the rabbinic courts could no longer help.

As personable as she is intellectual, Rachel uses both these traits in her work. One example:

"Back in roughly 2003, a convert wanted a divorce from her husband, who—in addition to never bathing—believed he was *Mashiach ben Yosef*. The husband refused to dissolve the marriage, because he thought it would disgrace the Messiah to be divorced. The court imprisoned him and even confiscated his *tallit* and *tefillin*, but to no avail. He was mentally ill, so he thought he'd been kidnapped and jailed unjustly.

"As an emissary of the *beit din*, I met with him. Very matter-of-factly, I showed him the court order requiring him to give his wife a *get*. He denied the document's authenticity and left the room.

"Afterward, I asked the prison rabbi for a tour, including the ward in which this husband was incarcerated. When he saw me, he asked if we could speak. Since he was completely asocial, this was highly unusual, and I seized the opportunity. I knew no one had treated him normally for years, so I decided I would. I started making small talk: 'You're from Brooklyn? Me too! Do you know…?' He didn't respond, so I went on chatting and smiling non-stop for 20 minutes. He listened attentively, and I sensed I had broken through. Finally, since it was around Rosh HaShanah, I asked him if he'd like to call his parents and wish them a happy new year, which he did. All this brought him back to reality somewhat, although he still considered himself *Mashiach*.

"Meanwhile, I and a colleague had been doing some research and discovered a major question about his wife's conversion—and therefore about his children's Jewishness. After giving him time to internalize our visit, we relayed this information to the chief justice, who in turn hinted to him that, if the case dragged on, the court might look into his wife's background. Having reconnected with reality, he understood that his children not being Jewish would disgrace the Messiah far more than divorce. So he gave the *get*."

To popularize prenuptial agreements, Rachel decided to author a scholarly work on the topic. "Although I had begun a doctorate in Talmud, I put off my dissertation for a few years, since I thought this book would do more good for the Jewish people than my Ph.D.," she tells me. Yet she wrote it in secret, anticipating opposition to the idea of a woman producing such a work.

In 2009, the Ariel Torah Institute published Rachel's book, *Spare Your Eyes Tears: Prenuptial Agreements for the Prevention of Get Refusal* (in Hebrew). The late Rabbi She'ar

Yashuv Cohen, then head of the Haifa Rabbinical Court, called it "the first responsum authored by a woman in Jewish history." A thousand copies were sent to rabbis all over the country. As expected, some had difficulty accepting it, or even believing a woman had written it.

Rachel was right to have prioritized her book. It continues to have a tremendous impact upon rabbis, judges, and lay scholars.

Soon after the book's publication, she earned her Ph.D.,

writing her dissertation on Israel's toughest cases of *get* refusal. Around the same time, she left the *Agunah* Unit but continuing counseling *agunot*.

In August 2013, based upon many recommendations, the justice minister appointed Rachel to a three-year-term on the State Commission for the Appointment of Rabbinical Court Judges. It was the highest position a woman had ever reached in the Israeli religious establishment. She now had the power to interview and assess any rabbi seeking to preside over a rabbinic court or be promoted from a regional court to the High Court.

"Interviews with other commission members would last around 15 minutes," Rachel informs me. "But I sat with applicants for up to two and a half hours, questioning them in halachah and then presenting actual scenarios and asking how they'd rule. They'd never been tested like that. They walked away stunned. Word got out that if candidates were to be interviewed by me, they'd better prepare—including studying my book. That's one way *Spare Your Eyes Tears* began to make inroads in religious society."

Rachel has represented approximately 100 women in court and has won nearly every case. She has advised hundreds more. She's also the first rabbinic advocate of her time—male or female—to persuade the court to coerce a husband by any means possible—including imprisonment—to give a *get*.

Presently, Rachel directs the *Agunot* and *Get* Refusal Prevention Project of the International Young Israel Movement in Israel. She has published over 170 articles in both the academic and popular press, participated in rabbinic forums, and lectured all over the Jewish world—and she has no intention of stopping. Needless to say, she also continues to advise and assist *agunot*. Not surprisingly, she has received numerous awards and fellowships.

Perhaps Rachel's greatest professional achievement is her promotion of prenuptial agreements. (She even consulted a psychologist in wording the one she coauthored.) Despite their clear, life-saving benefits, however, she still encounters resistance. How does Rachel pitch a prenup to a blissfully engaged couple who are sure they'll never need one? "I mention three important considerations," she says. "First, one never knows what the future may bring, so it pays to be protected. Second, the couple's friends may need one, so if they themselves set an example, others may follow their lead. Third, this is a once-in-a-lifetime opportunity to improve halachic processes. In signing a prenuptial agreement, couples are making history."

Although Rachel has been a trailblazer, she's no militant. She even broke with a major women's organization because it opposes the rabbinic establishment. Yet she challenges authority figures whenever necessary, demanding that they do everything in their power to effect justice.

"When God gave us the Torah, He also gave us the tools to work with it," Rachel states. "Religious leaders must ensure that the Torah remains vital. This task may require innovation within Jewish law. To me, that's the job of judges in the religious court system—to use their immense knowledge of Torah and the tools they've been given to solve our most pressing problems."

While endlessly devoted to helping *agunot*, Rachel also revels in her grandmother role. And though her high school and college hobby of crocheting has long gone by the wayside, she still manages to host large Shabbat meals for family, friends, and other guests.

Most of the time, however, she's working. "I've been privileged to study Torah on the highest level ever available to women in Jewish history," Rachel notes, "and that's a huge responsibility. Lives actually depend on my efforts. In addition, I often serve as a role model to young women. So even though my work can be tiring, I can't stop."

The title of Rachel's book, *Spare Your Eyes Tears*, is taken from Jeremiah 31:15, in which God tells the matriarch Rachel not to cry over her children's exile, because her work will be rewarded and they will return to their borders. "Yirmeyahu's words speak to me because Rachel acted, and her actions had an effect," Rachel says. "For me, that means that I—another 'Rachel'—also have to do whatever I can. And I hope my work too will be rewarded."

> When Rabbi Yochanan ben Zakkai was on his deathbed, his students said to him, "Our teacher—bless us!" He said, "Would that the fear of Heaven be upon you as much as the fear of human beings [which is far less important]." (Babylonian Talmud, Berachot 28b)

Chapter Seventeen

In Memoriam: From Cancer to Health

WHEN MY MOTHER was in her 40s, she was diagnosed with Hodgkin's lymphoma. She underwent radiation, and after five years with no recurrence, she was pronounced cured.

Some years later, however, cancer was discovered in her breast. Then in her colon. Then in her lung. Her heartbeat also weakened. Fortunately, all three cancers were detected early and removed. For her heart, a pacemaker was implanted.

Then, at age 75, she developed congenital heart failure. She underwent open-heart surgery to replace a faulty valve, but shortly afterward it became infected, requiring another operation. This time she didn't have the strength to recover.

After she died, her surgeon said he could tell from her bones that she'd been irradiated, and that the radiation had most likely caused her last three cancers and quite possibly her heart problems.

So radiation saved my mother's life. Yet had any of her subsequent cancers gone undetected, it could also have killed her. In the end, it may have caused her death. We'll never know.

Conventional cancer treatments are a double-edged sword. They can extend and even save lives. Yet they take a huge toll on the body. Chemotherapy destroys the immune system (a friend of mine undergoing chemo died not from her cancer but from a simple virus that her body had no strength to fight off). And radiation can do untold damage, including inducing new cancers. Is there no other way of treating the disease?

After losing his son to cancer, one man found such a way.

Abraham Safirstein (of blessed memory) was born in 1947 and raised in the Orthodox community of Buenos Aires. After marrying at age 19, he studied business, biology, and biochemistry. Over the years, he and his wife had four children and enjoyed a normal, happy family life.

In 1993, however, while living in North Miami Beach, the Safirsteins were dealt a tremendous blow. Their oldest son, newlywed Ariel, age 24, was diagnosed with brain cancer. He immediately underwent surgery to remove the tumor. Because his cancer was a rare sort immune to chemotherapy, his oncologist recommended a high dose of radiation to prevent recurrence, which Ariel also underwent.

Eighteen months later, the tumor reappeared. Again it was surgically removed. But Ariel had already received the maximum amount of radiation a person is allowed in his or her lifetime. So other than more surgery, his oncologist had nothing to offer.

Determined to heal his son, Abraham took matters into his own hands. He investigated various off-label chemotherapies, but their survival rates were abysmal, and the attendant health risks considerable.

Yet there was a bigger issue. Abraham realized that conventional cancer treatments treat the symptom, not the cause. They don't answer the crucial question of how and why cancer develops in the first place. Even if the disease can be made to disappear, therefore, it will likely return—often with a vengeance.

As a religious man, Abraham was accustomed to saying the blessing that acknowledges God's "fashioning the human being with wisdom." If we could tap that wisdom, he believed, the body could heal itself. With that, this father declared war on his son's cancer.

Every day after work, Abraham stayed up until two or three in the morning researching cancer on the Internet. Interested only in hard evidence, he limited himself to articles in peer-reviewed medical journals, double-checking all sources and calculations. He studied with a top pathologist to understand cancer cells' strengths and weaknesses. He learned everything he could from cutting-edge health practitioners. Then a doctor in his synagogue who had lost his wife to leukemia introduced him to the world of nutrition.

Abraham came to attribute cancer to a weakened immune system, chronic inflammation, hormonal imbalance, and toxins—and particularly to nutritional deficiencies. He believed he could reverse most of that through diet and supplements. A treatment program was taking shape in his mind.

Then Ariel's high-dose radiation reared its ugly head. A new, extremely aggressive cancer developed in the irradiated area of his brain. That's when Abraham learned that the radiation his son had received is successful in only 17% of cases and highly likely to result in another tumor within 8 to 12 years—which is exactly what happened.

Within a year, Ariel passed away.

After Ariel's death in 2001, the Safirsteins moved to Chicago. By now Abraham had been researching cancer for eight years. Although he couldn't save his son, he still hoped to help others. After another five years of study, he believed he understood how cancer works and how to defeat it naturally.

It wasn't long before Abraham's new program was put to the test. In 2007, his 85-year-old mother was diagnosed with stage 4 endometrial (uterine) cancer. She underwent a hysterectomy, but the cancer had metastasized. Neither chemotherapy nor radiation had ever worked in a case like hers, said her oncologist, recommending each nonetheless. Understandably, Mrs. Safirstein refused to submit to this regimen and its attendant suffering with no real hope of success. She was given 12–18 months to live.

Abraham proposed that his mother give his program a try. She agreed. Two months later, she had a CT scan. The cancer was gone. Her doctor, dumbfounded, was sure it would soon return. It didn't. Mrs. Safirstein stayed on the program, and to this day, at age 97, she's cancer-free.

Word got out, and people began calling Abraham from all over the world. Some had been given only months to live, but by following his treatment plan, many stabilized, improved, or went into remission. Eventually he quit his job and devoted himself fulltime to his new calling.

Abraham didn't just dispense supplements—he offered a caring heart and a sympathetic ear to families ravaged by cancer. "Having been in that vulnerable position myself—being caught completely off guard by a frightening diagnosis I could barely comprehend—I understand the helplessness and fear," he wrote on his website. "I share my knowledge and provide the type of valuable information I wish I had been armed with to battle the enemy and prevail. It has been rewarding for me to see people who've completely lost hope regain their health contrary to all expectations."

The Safirstein Program uses nutrients to rebuild the immune system and block cancer's energy supply. Two simple examples:

Cell functions are controlled by genes such as P53, which is responsible for apoptosis, or programmed cell death. Cancer turns this gene off, allowing diseased cells to proliferate. Vitamin D (actually a hormone) turns it on. Most cancer patients have very low vitamin D levels. High doses of vitamin D are therefore essential to Abraham's method.

Cancer cells also feed on glucose, drawn in by receptors called galectins. A supplement known as Galectin Control neutralizes these receptors, thereby starving the cancer. This supplement too is included in the program.

Of course, preventing cancer is far better than treating it. According to Abraham, just four nutrients—vitamin D, vitamin K-2 (as MK-4), iodine, and omega-3 fatty acids—can significantly reduce cancer risk.

Patients who've adopted Abraham's approach in conjunction with chemotherapy or radiation have suffered fewer side effects of those treatments. More important, these people regain the strength to fight cancer. "My husband's first month on chemo was terrible," a young woman told me. "He had no energy, no appetite, and felt awful. Then he tried the Safirstein Program. The change was remarkable. I got my husband back."

Abraham was in frequent contact with both MDs and naturopaths, all of whom were impressed by his knowledge. He had tremendous respect for them and vice versa.

On June 23, 2014, *Binah* magazine featured an article on Abraham entitled "Angel of Life," calling his program "an innovative, holistic therapeutic approach that deals with disease from the roots up." Since then, his work has gained fame in the Orthodox world and beyond.

Abraham Safirstein passed away in 2016. On the second anniversary of his death, his family wrote a moving tribute to him, praising his great dedication to others:

Beyond giving people his nutritional program, he gave them what he didn't have when he went through his own nightmare: clarity. He had all the time in the world for anyone who needed him—he would answer any questions, explain things as much as necessary, and tell [people] what to expect from conventional doctors, so the experience would be less frightening. He empowered [patients] to look at their options, so they could feel more in control instead of paralyzed and helpless. He was totally humble and unassuming, so everyone felt at ease with him; he was compassionate, so everyone felt cared for by him. He would bring his laptop on vacations and his phone on hikes, so he could always work and be available to people. His *ahavas Yisrael* knew no bounds.

I can attest to that. A few years ago, a family friend was treating his early-stage cancer solely with the Safirstein Program. Concerned yet intrigued, I met with Abraham while visiting the U.S. Unbeknownst to me, he was working 14-hour days, but he drove to where I was staying and spent a full hour with me, describing how his program works, showing me "before" and "after" images on his laptop, and patiently answering my questions. He was optimistic that our friend would recover. Abraham had even been praying for him, as he did for everyone on his program. (A few months later the cancer disappeared and has not returned.)

Needless to say, Abraham met with opposition. "People don't consider nutrition powerful enough to fight cancer," his wife told me. "So my husband would simply explain how the body works and the research behind his program. He didn't invent a remedy—he just took existing information and put it together in a new way. In any case, he never took credit for any success he had—he attributed it all to God."

No cancer treatment works for everyone, and Hashem ultimately holds the cards. Nevertheless, Abraham Safirstein restored hope to countless people. Rabbi Shmuel Kamenetsky called him "a great *shaliach* for *Klal Yisrael*." His family is continuing his work. May his program keep helping those in need, and may his memory be a blessing.

> The Tree of Life was in the center of the Garden of Eden (according to Rashi), because there is one central truth. At the same time, numerous points surround it, each equidistant from the center. All are valid ways of relating to truth. (Chafetz Chayim)

Chapter Eighteen

Dancing on the Edge

In winter 1999, the following article by "Batya Gold" (a pseudonym) appeared in Jewish Action:[*]

. . . .

THE ROOM IS packed to capacity. The noise is deafening. Working my way past the onlookers near the entrance, I manage to reach the outermost circle of dancing women. Someone notices me, takes my hand, and happily welcomes me into the crowd. The singing is unbelievably joyous as I add my voice to the countless others. I look around. Like every year, I wonder if I stand out, with my complete hair-covering, high neckline, below-the-elbow sleeves, long skirt, and stockings. On the other side of the shoulder-high *mechitzah*, I see the men's colorful *kippot serugot*, their shoulders bearing little boys waving flags. I love watching them.

---

[*] Reprinted with permission from *Jewish Action*, the quarterly magazine of the Orthodox Union, and slightly re-edited.

I wish my own black-yarmulked husband and sons were among them. But while the men's energy is wonderful, the spirit among the women is even higher. For there are few Orthodox places in Jerusalem where women can celebrate Simchas Torah like this—not just watching men sing and dance with *sifrei Torah*, but doing so themselves.

Simchas Torah is the time when I, a *charedi* woman, leave my community to seek religious expression elsewhere. This holiday reflects my struggle to find an outlet for a spiritual need unrecognized by the *charedi* world while still maintaining my affiliation with that world.

My feelings about Simchas Torah have moved through different phases. Eighteen years ago, coming to Judaism from a society that extolled androgyny, I was taken with the Torah's affirmation of women's right to be women and of a distinctly feminine spiritual path. On my first Simchas Torah, I repressed my resentment at being unable to participate by reminding myself that I didn't have to do what men do to achieve closeness to Hashem. By the time I was married and the mother of two small children, I had blocked out most of my negativity. As I stood outside the *beis midrash* with my youngest in my arms, watching through a window as my husband danced with our *bechor* on his shoulders, the fullness of wifehood and motherhood made it difficult to feel anything but joy.

But as the years passed, my feelings began to shift. I was still a spiritually centered *charedi* woman. I wanted neither to be a man nor to be Modern Orthodox. And perhaps, as apologists claimed, I had no need to celebrate as men do in order to love Hashem's Torah. But still, I longed to. It felt increasingly wrong that while I was actively learning Torah,

I was expected to be a passive bystander to its celebration. And even if I *weren't* studying Torah, I was living it. My soul, which had received the Torah with the rest of *Klal Yisrael* at Sinai, was thirsting for a more direct experience.

I decided to consult a highly respected *charedi* rabbi who might be sympathetic. I asked my *shailah*: May women celebrate as men do on Simchas Torah, dancing with a *sefer Torah?* His answer was negative.

I shared this disappointing but somewhat expected response with my friend Sarah Yehudit—a brilliant woman who spends most of her waking hours learning Torah and whose desire to actively celebrate Simchas Torah was even more burning than mine. She felt that had I prefaced my question with a clear explanation of my motivation, the answer might have been different. On behalf of both of us, she drafted a new *shailah*.

Dear Rabbi,

Simchas Torah has always been a complicated day for me, and for most women I know. I have wandered from shul to shul, trying to find a way of celebrating that feels right.

Women are supposed to participate vicariously by watching men dance and sing. Yet as women enter into a more direct relationship with Torah study, indirect participation on Simchas Torah no longer works for many of them. Instead of reinforcing one's bond to Torah, it creates alienation. Instead of *simchah*, it creates pain.

I love Torah and spend my days immersed in its study. I want to celebrate that on the day designated for celebration. For the past several years, I just sang and danced alone in my study, because it felt more real than anything else I could do.

There is an Orthodox learning center in Jerusalem called Yakar where women also dance with the Torah on their side of the *mechitzah*. This is not politically motivated. The *kehillah* has a rabbi who studied the question and ruled that the dancing was permissible. Many of the most serious and respected women teachers of Torah in Jerusalem attend. They're not making a feminist statement. They're just expressing their love of Torah. This, too, is my motivation. Batya Gold shares my feelings exactly.

In light of the above, we would like to reraise the question of women dancing with a *sefer Torah* in the hope that you might reconsider your answer. We thank you for your time, patience, and sensitivity.

A few days later, the rabbi spoke to Sarah Yehudit. He had read her letter. And he had changed his mind. At the same time, he uncharacteristically requested that we not tell anyone he was the source of our *pesak*. "I'm afraid it will be misinterpreted," he said sadly. "The practice of women dancing with a *sefer Torah* has come to be associated with opposition to normative Judaism. Still, your reasons are valid, and *emmes* is *emmes*. You may go to Yakar."

So the following year I found myself, accompanied by my two little daughters (and my husband's support), in a neighborhood far from my own, celebrating Simchas Torah at Yakar.

For six years now, I've gone. And it's always special, particularly because of the interesting mix of women. The majority are young and single: Modern Orthodox Americans,

Israeli *dati le'umi* girls, and in-process *ba'alos teshuvah* from anywhere and everywhere. But there are also older women, married and unmarried, mothers and children, and even grandmothers—as well as a number of prominent Jerusalem educators.

As usual, I work my way into the inner circle of dancers. Seeing the eagerness on my face, someone signals that I be given a *sefer Torah*. I take it carefully in my arms. I'm always nervous at first—what if I drop it, God forbid? But my fear subsides, and holding it close to me, I circle with it, almost shyly, in the midst of the singing and dancing women, feeling indescribable happiness.

Perhaps even greater are the elation and awe I feel watching other women hold the *sefer Torah*—some of them, like myself five years ago, for the first time. A young woman receives it with a huge smile and dances with it joyfully and freely. She gives it to a woman in her 50s who, accepting it graciously, bears it with regal dignity and pride. It next passes to Sarah Yehudit, who hugs it tightly for several moments, eyes shut in deep concentration; then she suddenly raises it above our heads, up and down, in all directions, with an intense exuberance. But the woman who always brings tears to my eyes is "Dina." A deeply spiritual teacher and mother of six, she simply radiates the joy of living, learning, and breathing Torah. Dina takes the *sefer Torah* in her arms and cradles it with the tenderness of a mother toward her newborn. Her cheek pressed softly against its velvet cover, she rocks gently to and fro, eyes closed, oblivious to the commotion around her, a look of pure bliss on her face.

One year after lunch, Dina and I take our children to a park. Dina is intrigued by the contradiction between my

presence at Yakar and my membership in the *charedi* community. I admit that celebrating Simchas Torah at Yakar meets
a spiritual need that would otherwise remain unfulfilled.

Sensing my openness, Dina decides to be direct. She
doesn't attack, just honestly questions. "Why do you identify with the *charedim*?" she wants to know. "Spiritually, they
have no positive outlook on change, no creativity, no ability
to meet challenges other than by just pulling in. What do
you see in that world?"

Rather than debate the accuracy of her statement, I go to
the heart of the issue for me. "There's a kind of purity there
that's hard to find," I answer. "A different quality of *tznius*, of
mesirus nefesh. A more intense *yiras Shamayim*."

I sense that Dina understands, but she isn't ready to
concede. "There are different kinds of *yirat Shamayim*," she
points out. "Maybe you know how to recognize only one."

Maybe, I think to myself. But that kind stirs something
so deep in me...

Later, I ask Sarah Yehudit whether she feels as negatively
as Dina about the *charedi* world. "No," she answers soberly,
"I don't." Shaking her head slowly, she says quietly, "There's
definitely something special there."

Yes. There's definitely something special there. How I
wish I could celebrate Simchas Torah as I do at Yakar with
my own neighbors. Several respected *charedi* women have
privately confessed that they would love to. One well-known
rebbetzin has refrained from going to Yakar only because
people might draw the wrong conclusions about her *hashkafah*. What seems so normal and legitimate to some of us
is still feared by many others. Meanwhile, I'm the only one

who feels strongly enough to actually step out. Clearly, I'm a misfit. Someday things will change. But it's so hard to wait.

I voice my frustration to the rabbi and ask what can be done to expedite the process. "A bold change isn't *tzanua*," he says. "Change in the Jewish world has to happen slowly, organically."

Sarah Yehudit disagrees. "No change initially happens 'organically,'" she says. "It happens because some group of people 'boldly' breaks with established practice. Then others follow, and gradually more and more do, until the change becomes 'organically' accepted. But there's always an initial break." Sarah Yehudit sighs. "I'm not brave enough to join that group of leaders, but I thank God for them."

With two of my daughters now in the *charedi* school system, I wonder how long I'll be brave enough even to remain a follower. I live in one world yet have a foot in another. I want the traditional *tznius*, the *taharah*, the *temimus* that are such rare and precious commodities outside the Jerusalem *charedi* community (and, increasingly, even within it)—yet I also want to actively celebrate my connection to and love of Torah. And while I don't know how much longer I'll be able to bring my daughters to Yakar—or go myself—I want this for them too. I pray that one day they'll have it all, in one world, without the conflict I find so painful.

Only once have I experienced the absence of that conflict. I'll never forget that glorious, golden moment. It was my first Simchas Torah at Yakar. Sarah Yehudit was holding my three-year-old daughter, Temima, and another woman had taken one-year-old Emuna so I could dance with the *sefer Torah*. Athough thrilled, I felt somewhat unnatural in this new role. Suddenly I saw Emuna crying for me.

Automatically, I shifted the full weight of the *sefer Torah* onto my right arm and took her with my left. She immediately stopped crying and snuggled close to me.

There I stood, a *sefer Torah* in one arm and my precious baby in the other. All sense of conflict evaporated as both sides of me were simultaneously affirmed: Torah study and celebration alongside motherhood. Change alongside tradition. A warm feeling of peace washed over me, the deepest I had experienced for a long time. I pray it will someday settle over my whole life.

....

I am the author of this article.

Sarah Yehudit and I have continued to celebrate Simchat Torah together every year, most often at Yakar. An entire generation has passed since we first began attending, and some interesting changes have occurred.

Back in 1994, Orthodox women dancing with Torah scrolls was a new phenomenon, and Yakar was virtually the only Orthodox synagogue in Jerusalem offering the opportunity. Well-known female educators came from all over to take part. Before the *hakafot*, Rebbetzin Gilla Rosen—whose husband Mickey, of blessed memory, was Yakar's rabbi—gave a talk explaining why (based on rabbinic sources) women were permitted to dance with a *sefer Torah*. The participants were of all ages, many with a distinctly "alternative" look, and most of the tunes sung were those of Shlomo Carlebach.

Today these teachers can probably dance in synagogues closer to home. There's no longer any need for an explanatory class. And while the women at Yakar are still wonderfully diverse, the majority are conventional young *dati le'umi* women who've grown up celebrating Simchat Torah this way.

One year, Sarah Yehudit and I spent Simchat Torah at the women's seminary in Bat Ayin, a community in Gush Etzion. It was the first year the students were given a *sefer Torah* to dance with. I still remember the prefatory words of the seminary's director, Rabbi Natan Greenberg. "This is a new female experience," he told us. "Don't feel you have to imitate the men. Let your singing and dancing emerge from who you are spiritually as women." Indeed, for one of the seven *hakafot*, rather than dancing to a lively tune, we sang a slow, soulful melody with our arms around one another.

The observance of Simchat Torah has changed over the years, and so have I. I still live in a largely *charedi* neighborhood. I love many things about the *charedi* community and maintain many *charedi* values. Yet I find it's meaningful to draw from other parts of the Orthodox world as well. Consequently, it's sometimes hard to label myself. It seems easier to identify simply as a Jew who loves God, loves Torah, and is committed to mitzvot.

Like all those profiled in this book, I've learned that few things in life feel better than accepting and being myself.

> Human existence used to be simpler. People lived in a particular place and belonged to a fairly homogeneous community. But now we're patchwork souls, cobbling together our various facets and affinities. Consequently, our "home" is best imagined not as a point but as a smear, and our community is a more complex terrain. We do have a place

in the universe, but it is uniquely our own—and as such, it's just about as perfect as can be. (Sarah Yehudit Schneider)

Afterword

In her book *More Time to Think*, Nancy Kline recounts the following story:

When I was 17, I discovered a wonderful thing. My father and I were sitting on the floor of his study. We were organizing his old papers. Across the carpet I saw a fat paper clip. Its rust dusted the cover sheet of a report of some kind. I picked it up. I started to read. Then I started to cry.

It was a speech he had written in 1920, in Tennessee. Then only 17 himself and graduating from high school, he had called for equality for African Americans. I marveled, proud of him, and wondered how, in 1920, so young, so white, and in the Deep South, he had had the courage to deliver it.

"Daddy," I said, handing him the pages, "this speech—how did you ever get permission to give it? And weren't you scared?"

"Well, honey," he said, "I didn't ask for permission. I just asked myself, 'What is the most important challenge facing my generation?' I knew immediately.

"Then I asked myself, 'And if I weren't afraid, what would I say about it in this speech?'

"I wrote it. And I delivered it. About halfway through I looked out to see the entire audience of faculty, students and parents stand up—and walk out. Left alone on the stage, I thought to myself, 'Well, I guess I need to be sure to do only two things with my life: keep thinking for myself, and not get killed.'"

He handed the speech back to me and smiled. "I seem to have done both," he said.

"Thank you," I said.

I had no idea then just how much I was thanking him for. I knew he had set aside fear to be a person of conviction. That was plenty. But he had also been a person thinking for himself by asking powerful questions and listening to the answers.

I learned courage and integrity from him that day. But I also learned that doing your own thinking is the first step in making a difference.

We may never make a public speech in which the entire audience walks out. But the point of this story is being able to think for ourselves and stand up for what we believe in. First and foremost, we must think about who we are and believe we can be ourselves.

Being ourselves in the Orthodox world requires several things:

- studying God's handbook for living, the Torah
- knowing what our souls want and what we feel passionate about
- recognizing our talents and abilities
- seeking good advice about where to put our energies

In addition, we need the following:

+ the integrity to ask ourselves powerful questions and listen to the answers

+ the courage to go—with appropriate spiritual guidance—where those answers lead us

If we end up being "out of the box," we may encounter social pressure to be like everyone else, leaving us wondering how to be part of a community while maintaining our individuality. Maybe it's actually not that hard. If we make it clear that we really identify with and care about our community, going out of our way to conform where we can, the community will likely accept us as is.* Those around us may even come to appreciate and learn from our differences—just as we should all learn from each other.

The beloved Chassidic personality Rabbi Zusha of Anipoli famously said: "In the next world, I won't be asked, 'Why weren't you Moses?' I'll be asked, 'Why weren't you Zusha?'" In the future, looking back on our lives, may we be able to say: "I was myself."

---

* Moishe Bane, "Recalibration," *Klal Perspectives*, February 12, 2015.

Acknowledgments

AN ENORMOUS, HEARTFELT thanks to all the amazing individuals who gave me the honor of including them in this book and answered countless questions so I could do them justice. It was a privilege to enter your world, and I loved every minute of writing about you.

A huge thank-you to my loving and insightful husband, Avraham, for helping shape the introduction and afterword, and for his incisive comments on the entire book.

I am indebted to a dear, special friend (who wishes to remain anonymous) for moderating me, censoring me when necessary, and helping me present the Jewish world with a book that I hope and pray will be a *kiddush Hashem*.

My deep appreciation to Rabbi Yitzchak Breitowitz, *shlita*, and to Rabbi Yitzchak Berkovits, *shlita*, for believing in this book and honoring it with their beautiful approbations.

Most of all, of course, my endless gratitude to Hashem for giving me such a rewarding life, full of meaning, purpose, and wonderful people: my family, friends, students, and more. I am truly blessed.

Glossary

All terms are Hebrew unless otherwise stated.

ahavas Yisrael – love of one's fellow Jews

alef-bet – Hebrew alphabet

aliyah – immigration to Israel

Am Yisrael – the Jewish people

avodah zarah – idol worship

avodat Hashem – service of God

avrechim – young, married yeshivah students

ba'al teshuvah (pl. *ba'alei teshuvah*) – a (male) Jew who has returned to religious observance

ba'alot (or *ba'alos*) *teshuvah* – Jewish girls or women who have returned to religious observance

Bais Yaakov – right-wing Orthodox educational system for girls

bar mitzvah – 13-year-old boy's religious coming of age (lit. mitzvah boy)

baruch Hashem – thank God (lit. blessed is God)

bat mitzvah – 12-year-old girl's religious coming of age (lit. mitzvah girl) *bechor* – firstborn son

beit (or *beis*) *midrash* – study hall

beit din – rabbinic court

b'nei Torah – Torah-centered men, usually studying full-time in yeshivah

B'nei Yisrael – the Children of Israel

bashert (Yiddish) – meant to be (lit. intended)

brachah – blessing

bris – ritual circumcision (lit. covenant)

bubby (Yiddish) – grandma

chagim – festivals

challah – traditional braided bread eaten on Shabbat

charedi (pl. *charedim*) – right-wing Orthodox

chasan – bridegroom

Chassidim – Chassidic Jews

Chassidish – Chassidic

Chassidut – Chassidic thought

chavruta (or *chavrusa*) – study partner

cheder – right-wing Orthodox elementary school for boys

chesed – kindness

Chol HaMoed – intermediate days of a festival

chozrim bit'shuvah – Jews who've returned to religious observance

chug – extracurricular activity (lit. circle)

Chumash – Five Books of Moses

chuppah – wedding ceremony (lit. canopy)

dati leumi – religious Zionist

daven (Yiddish) – pray

davkanik – contrary person

derech – (religious) path

devar Torah (pl. *divrei Torah*) – brief Torah idea (lit. word of Torah)

d'oraisa – originating in the Written Torah

emmes – truth

erev – eve

eruv – ritual enclosure converting an area into a private domain

frum (Yiddish) – religious

frumkeit (Yiddish) – religiosity

gedolim – great rabbis

gehinnom – hell

Gemara – Talmud

Haggadot – texts read at the *seder*

HaKadosh Baruch Hu – the Holy One, Blessed Be He (God)

hakafot – circle dancing with Torah scrolls on Simchat Torah

halachah – Jewish law

Hashem – God

hashkafah – religious/philosophical outlook

hitbodedut – talking in seclusion with God

issur – prohibition

Kabbalah – Jewish mysticism

kashrut – dietary laws

kavanah – intention

kefirah – heresy

kehillah – community

kiddush – blessing over wine recited at the start of a Shabbat or festive meal

kiddush Hashem – act that reflects well on Torah Judaism (lit. sanctification of God's name)

kippot serugot – knitted yarmulkes

kiruv – outreach to non-religious Jews

kiyum – fulfillment

Klal Yisrael – the Jewish people

kollel – yeshivah for married men

Kotel – Western Wall

lehavdil – to make a distinction (between holy and mundane)

madrichah – group counselor

Mashiach ben Yosef – Messiah son of Joseph, preceding the Messiah from the house of David

mazal tov – congratulations (lit. good fortune)

mechitzah – partition

Megillot Ester – Scrolls of Esther, containing the text of the biblical book of Esther

menorah – candelabrum

meshugas (Yiddish) – craziness

mesirut (or *mesirus*) *nefesh* – self-sacrifice

Midrash – ancient Bible commentary

mikveh – ritual bath

mitzvah (pl. *mitzvot*) – commandment or good deed

moshav – farming community

mutar – permitted

neshamah – soul

nisyonos – trials or tribulations

parashah (pl. *parashiyot*) – weekly Torah portion

Pesach – Passover

pesak – Jewish legal ruling

posek – Jewish legal authority

rav (pl. *rabbanim*) – rabbi

rebbe – spiritual teacher

rebbetzin (Yiddish) – rabbi's wife (or any woman of distinction)

Rosh HaShanah – Jewish New Year

rosh kollel – head of a *kollel*

seder – ritual Passover meal

sefer (pl. *sefarim*) – Torah book

sefer Torah (pl. *sifrei Torah*) – Torah scroll

semichah – rabbinic ordination

Shabbat (or *Shabbos*; pl. *Shabbatot*) – the Sabbath

shalach manos – food gifts given on the holiday of Purim

shaliach – agent (of God)

shailah – question

sheitel – wig

shidduchim – marital matches

shiurim – Torah classes

shlita – "may he live a good long life, Amen"

shomer Shabbat – Sabbath observer

shtiebelach (Yiddish) – small, informal places, often Chassidic, used for communal prayer

shul (Yiddish) – synagogue

siddur – prayer book

simchah – joy or joyous occasion

Simchat (or *Simchas*) *Torah* – festival marking the end and new beginning of the annual cycle of Torah readings

taharah – purity

tallit – prayer shawl

talmid chacham – Torah scholar (lit. student of a wise man)

talmid muvhak – close disciple (lit. outstanding student)

Tanach – Bible

tefillah – prayer

tefillin – phylacteries, i.e. small, leather boxes containing biblical texts and worn by a man on his head and arm during morning prayer

temimus – innocence, wholesomeness

tikkun olam – rectification of the world

Torah – (1) the Five Books of Moses; (2) Judaism or Jewish teachings

tzaddik – righteous man

tzanua – modest

tzniut (or *tznius*) – modesty

yerei Shamayim – God-fearing (lit. fearful of Heaven)

yeshivah (pl. *yeshivot*) – Jewish study center for males

yeshivish – connected to the yeshivah world

Yiddishkeit (Yiddish) – Judaism

yimach shemam – "may their names be blotted out"

Yirmeyahu – Jeremiah

yirat (or *yiras*) *Shamayim* – fear of Heaven (sincere religiosity)

Yom Tov – festival (lit. good day)

Zohar – seminal work of Jewish mysticism

About the Author

Gila Manolson (née Marilyn Fisch) grew up in the northeastern United States and attended Yale University, where she majored in music and graduated *magna cum laude*. After coming to Israel, she studied at Neve Yerushalayim College for Women, then later at Midreshet Rachel and Nishmat. For five years, she was the resident supervisor of the women's Heritage House, a Jewish outreach youth hostel in Jerusalem's Old City. An international speaker, Gila has also authored four other books for the Jewish world—which have been translated into several languages—and one for non-Jews. She is also a certified life coach. She and her husband, Avraham, live in Jerusalem and are the parents of seven children.

Gila's website is www.gilamanolson.com.